YO-ABE-513

AS-14

5/13

New and Selected Poems: 1962–2012

ALSO BY CHARLES SIMIC

New and Selected

Poems $\left\{\dfrac{1962}{2012}\right\}$

CHARLES SIMIC

Houghton Mifflin Harcourt
Boston   New York   2013

For information about permission to reproduce selections from this book,
write to Permissions, Houghton Mifflin Harcourt Publishing Company,
215 Park Avenue South, New York, New York 10003.

www.hmhbooks.com

Library of Congress Cataloging-in-Publication Data
Simic, Charles, date.
[Poems. Selections]
New and selected poems 1962/2012 / Charles Simic.
    pages cm
ISBN 978-0-547-92828-9
I. Title.
PS3569.I4725N49 2013
811'.54 — dc23   2012042188

Book design by Greta Sibley

Printed in the United States of America

DOC 10 9 8 7 6 5 4 3 2 1

for Abigail

CONTENTS

from Selected Early Poems

from Unending Blues

from *The World Doesn't End*

from The Book of Gods and Devils

from Hotel Insomnia

from A Wedding in Hell

from Walking the Black Cat

from Jackstraws

from Night Picnic

from My Noiseless Entourage

from That Little Something

from Master of Disguises

from The Voice at 3:00 A.M.

New Poems

from Selected Early Poems

Butcher Shop

Sometimes walking late at night
I stop before a closed butcher shop.
There is a single light in the store
Like the light in which the convict digs his tunnel.

An apron hangs on the hook:
The blood on it smeared into a map
Of the great continents of blood,
The great rivers and oceans of blood.

There are knives that glitter like altars
In a dark church
Where they bring the cripple and the imbecile
To be healed.

There is a wooden block where bones are broken,
Scraped clean—a river dried to its bed
Where I am fed,
Where deep in the night I hear a voice.

Cockroach

When I see a cockroach,
I don't grow violent like you.
I stop as if a friendly greeting
Had passed between us.

■

This roach is familiar to me.
We met here and there,
In the kitchen at midnight,
And now on my pillow.

■

I can see it has a couple
Of my black hairs
Sticking out of its head,
And who knows what else?

■

It carries a false passport—
Don't ask me how I know.
A false passport, yes,
With my baby picture.

Tapestry

It hangs from heaven to earth.
There are trees in it, cities, rivers,
small pigs and moons. In one corner
the snow falling over a charging cavalry,
in another women are planting rice.

You can also see:
a chicken carried off by a fox,
a naked couple on their wedding night,
a column of smoke,
an evil-eyed woman spitting into a pail of milk.

What is behind it?
—Space, plenty of empty space.

And who is talking now?
—A man asleep under his hat.

What happens when he wakes up?
—He'll go into a barbershop.
They'll shave his beard, nose, ears, and hair,
To make him look like everyone else.

Evening

The snail gives off stillness.
The weed is blessed.
At the end of a long day
The man finds joy, the water peace.

Let all be simple. Let all stand still
Without a final direction.
That which brings you into the world
To take you away at death
Is one and the same;
The shadow long and pointy
Is its church.

At night some understand what the grass says.
The grass knows a word or two.
It is not much. It repeats the same word
Again and again, but not too loudly . . .

The Inner Man

It isn't the body
That's a stranger.
It's someone else.

We poke the same
Ugly mug
At the world.
When I scratch,
He scratches too.

There are women
Who claim to have held him.
A dog follows me about.
It might be his.

If I'm quiet, he's quieter.
So I forget him.
Yet, as I bend down
To tie my shoelaces,
He's standing up.

We cast a single shadow.
Whose shadow?
I'd like to say:
"He was in the beginning
And he'll be in the end,"
But one can't be sure.

At night
As I sit
Shuffling the cards of our silence,
I say to him:

"Though you utter
Every one of my words,
You are a stranger.
It's time you spoke."

Fear

Fear passes from man to man
Unknowing,
As one leaf passes its shudder
To another.

All at once the whole tree is trembling,
And there is no sign of the wind.

Summer Morning

I love to stay in bed
All morning,
Covers thrown off, naked,
Eyes closed, listening.

Outside they are opening
Their primers
In the little school
Of the cornfield.

There's a smell of damp hay,
Of horses, laziness,
Summer sky and eternal life.

I know all the dark places
Where the sun hasn't reached yet,
Where the last cricket
Has just hushed; anthills
Where it sounds like it's raining;
Slumbering spiders spinning wedding dresses.

I pass over the farmhouses
Where the little mouths open to suck,
Barnyards where a man, naked to the waist,
Washes his face and shoulders with a hose,
Where the dishes begin to rattle in the kitchen.

The good tree with its voice
Of a mountain stream
Knows my steps.
It, too, hushes.

I stop and listen:
Somewhere close by
A stone cracks a knuckle,
Another rolls over in its sleep.

I hear a butterfly stirring
Inside a caterpillar,
I hear the dust talking
Of last night's storm.

Farther ahead, someone
Even more silent
Passes over the grass
Without bending it.

And all of a sudden!
In the midst of that quiet,
It seems possible
To live simply on this earth.

Dismantling the Silence

Take down its ears first,
Carefully, so they don't spill over.
With a sharp whistle slit its belly open.
If there are ashes in it, close your eyes
And blow them whichever way the wind is pointing.
If there's water, sleeping water,
Bring the root of a flower that hasn't drunk for a month.

When you reach the bones,
And you haven't got a dog with you,
And you haven't got a pine coffin
And a cart pulled by oxen to make them rattle,
Slip them quickly under your skin.
Next time you hunch your shoulders
You'll feel them pressing against your own.

It is now pitch-dark.
Slowly and with patience
Search for its heart. You will need
To crawl far into the empty heavens
To hear it beat.

Bestiary for the Fingers of My Right Hand

1

Thumb, loose tooth of a horse.
Rooster to his hens.
Horn of a devil. Fat worm
They have attached to my flesh
At the time of my birth.
It takes four to hold him down,
Bend him in half, until the bone
Begins to whimper.

Cut him off. He can take care
Of himself. Take root in the earth,
Or go hunting with wolves.

The second points the way.
True way. The path crosses the earth,
The moon and some stars.
Watch, he points further.
He points to himself.

The middle one has backache.
Stiff, still unaccustomed to this life;
An old man at birth. It's about something
That he had and lost,
That he looks for within my hand,
The way a dog looks
For fleas
With a sharp tooth.

4

The fourth is a mystery.
Sometimes as my hand
Rests on the table
He jumps by himself
As though someone called his name.

After each bone, finger,
I come to him, troubled.

5

Something stirs in the fifth,
Something perpetually at the point
Of birth. Weak and submissive,
His touch is gentle.
It weighs a tear.
It takes the mote out of the eye.

Fork

This strange thing must have crept
Right out of hell.
It resembles a bird's foot
Worn around the cannibal's neck.

As you hold it in your hand,
As you stab with it into a piece of meat,
It is possible to imagine the rest of the bird:
Its head which like your fist
Is large, bald, beakless, and blind.

Spoon

An old spoon,
Chewed
And licked clean,

Fixing you
With its evil-eyed
Stare,

As you lean over
The soup bowl
On the table,

To make sure
Once more
There is nothing left.

Knife

1

Father-confessor
Of the fat hen
On the red altar
Of its throat,

A tongue,
All alone,
Bringing the darkness of a mouth
Now lost.

A single shining eye
Of a madman—
If there's a tear in it,
Whom is it for?

2

It is a candle
It is also a track
Of crooked letters;
The knife's mysterious writings.

We go down
An inner staircase.
We walk under the earth.
The knife lights the way.

Through bones of animals,
Water, beard of a wild boar—
We go through stones, embers,
We are after a scent.

3

So much darkness
Everywhere.
We are in a bag
Slung
Over someone's shoulders.

You hear the sound
Of marching boots.
You hear the earth
Answering
With a hollow thud.

If it's a poem
You want,
Take a knife;

A star of solitude,
It will rise and set in your hand.

My Shoes

Shoes, secret face of my inner life:
Two gaping toothless mouths,
Two partly decomposed animal skins
Smelling of mice nests.

My brother and sister who died at birth
Continuing their existence in you,
Guiding my life
Toward their incomprehensible innocence.

What use are books to me
When in you it is possible to read
The Gospel of my life on earth
And still beyond, of things to come?

I want to proclaim the religion
I have devised for your perfect humility
And the strange church I am building
With you as the altar.

Ascetic and maternal, you endure:
Kin to oxen, to Saints, to condemned men,
With your mute patience, forming
The only true likeness of myself.

Thank you for using self-checkout!

RAGAP, CHELSEA M

0000417446
The human voice : how this extraordinary
instrument reveals essential clues about
who we are / by An
Date Due: 05-28-13

0000509467
New and selected poems 1962-2012 /
Charles Simic.
Date Due: 05-21-13

0000104367
The challenge of pain / Ronald Melzack and
Patrick D. Wall.
Date Due: 05-28-13

0000219264
The art of worldly wisdom : a pocket oracle /
Baltasar Gracian ; translated by Christopher
Maurer.
Date Due: 05-28-13

0000367031
Peter's quotations : ideas for our time / by
Laurence J. Peter.
Date Due: 05-28-13

Monday thru Thursday 9 A.M to 8 P.M.
Friday and Saturday 9 A.M. to 6 P.M.
Sunday 1 P.M. to 5 P.M.
970-962-2665
WWW.LOVELANDPUBLICLIBRARY.ORG
No. Checked Out / No. Not Checked Out
5 / 0

Stone

Go inside a stone
That would be my way.
Let somebody else become a dove
Or gnash with a tiger's tooth.
I am happy to be a stone.

From the outside the stone is a riddle:
No one knows how to answer it.
Yet within, it must be cool and quiet
Even though a cow steps on it full weight,
Even though a child throws it in a river;
The stone sinks, slow, unperturbed
To the river bottom
Where the fishes come to knock on it
And listen.

I have seen sparks fly out
When two stones are rubbed,
So perhaps it is not dark inside after all;
Perhaps there is a moon shining
From somewhere, as though behind a hill —
Just enough light to make out
The strange writings, the star charts
On the inner walls.

Poem Without a Title

I say to the lead,
"Why did you let yourself
Be cast into a bullet?
Have you forgotten the alchemists?
Have you given up hope
Of turning into gold?"

Nobody answers.
Lead. Bullet.
With names like that
The sleep is deep and long.

Concerning My Neighbors, the Hittites

Great are the Hittites.
Their ears have mice and mice have holes.
Their dogs bury themselves and leave the bones
To guard the house. A single weed holds all their storms
Until the spiderwebs spread over the heavens.
There are bits of straw in their lakes and rivers
Looking for drowned men. When a camel won't pass
Through the eye of one of their needles,
They tie a house to its tail. Great are the Hittites.
Their fathers are in cradles, their newborn make war.
To them lead floats, a leaf sinks. Their god is the size
Of a mustard seed so that he can be quickly eaten.

They also piss against the wind,
Pour water in a leaky bucket,
Strike two tears to make fire,
And have tongues with bones in them,
Bones of a wolf gnawed by lambs.

They are also called you only live once,
They are called a small leak
Will sink a great ship, they are called
Don't bite the hand that feeds you, they are called
You can't take it to the grave with you.

It's that hum in your left ear,
A sigh rising from deep within you,
A dream in which you keep falling forever,
The hour in which you sit up in bed
As though someone has called your name.

No one knows why the Hittites exist,
Still, when two are whispering
One of them is listening.

Did they catch the falling knife?
They caught it like a fly with closed mouths.
Did they balance the last egg?
They struck the egg with a bone so it won't howl.
Did they wait for dead man's shoes?
The shoes went in at one ear and out the other.
Did they wipe the blood from their mousetraps?

They burnt the blood to warm themselves.
Are they cold with no pockets in their shrouds?
If the sky falls, they shall have clouds for supper.

What do they have for us
To put in our pipes and smoke?
They have the braid of a beautiful girl
That drew a team of cattle
And the picture of him who slept
With dogs and rose with fleas
Searching for its trace in the sky.

■

And so, there are fewer and fewer of them now.
Who wrote their name on paper
And burnt the paper? Who put snake bones
In their pillows? Who threw nail parings
In their soup? Who made them walk
Under the ladder? Who stuck pins
In their snapshots?

The king of warts and his brother evil eye.
Bone-lazy and her sister rabbit's-foot.
Cross-your-fingers and their father dog star.
Knock-on-wood and his mother hellfire.

Because the tail can't wag the cow.
Because the woods can't fly to the dove.
Because the stones haven't said their last word.
Because dunghills rise and empires fall.

■

They are leaving behind
All the silver spoons
Found inside their throats at birth,
A hand they bit because it fed them,
Two rats from a ship that is still sinking,
A collection of various split hairs,
The leaf they turned over too late.

Here comes a forest in wolf's clothing,
The wise hen bows to the umbrella.
When the bloodshot evening meets the bloodshot night,
They tell each other bloodshot tales.

That bare branch over them speaks louder than words.
The moon is worn threadbare.

I repeat: lean days don't come singly,
It takes all kinds to make the sun rise.
The night is each man's castle.
Don't let the castle out of the bag.
Wind in the valley, wind in the high hills,
Practice will make this body fit this bed.

All roads lead
Out of a sow's ear
To what's worth
Two in the bush.

Invention of Nothing

I didn't notice
while I wrote here
that nothing remains of the world
except my table and chair.

And so I said:
(to hear myself talk)
Is this the tavern
without a glass, wine, or waiter
where I'm the long-awaited drunk?

The color of nothing is blue.
I strike it with my left hand and the hand disappears.
Why am I so quiet then
and so happy?

I climb on the table
(the chair is gone already)
I sing through the throat
of an empty beer bottle.

errata

Where it says snow
read teeth marks of a virgin
Where it says knife read
you passed through my bones
like a police whistle
Where it says table read horse
Where it says horse read my migrant's bundle

Apples are to remain apples
Each time a hat appears
think of Isaac Newton
reading the Old Testament
Remove all periods
They are scars made by words
I couldn't bring myself to say
Put a finger over each sunrise
it will blind you otherwise
That damn ant is still stirring
Will there be time left to list
all errors to replace
all hands guns owls plates
all cigars ponds woods and reach
that beer bottle my greatest mistake
the word I allowed to be written
when I should have shouted
her name

The Bird

A bird calls me
From a tall tree
In my dream,

Calls me from the pink twig of daylight,
From the long shadow
That inches each night closer to my heart,
Calls me from the edge of the world.

I give her my dream.
She dyes it red.
I give her my breath.
She turns it into rustling leaves.

She calls me from the highest cloud.
Her chirp
Like a match flickering
In a new grave.

■

Bird, shaped
Like the insides
Of a yawning mouth.

At daybreak,
When the sky turns clear and lucent
Like the water in which
They baptized a small child,
I climbed toward you.

The earth grew smaller underneath.
The howling emptiness
Chilled my feet,
And then my heart.

■

Later, I dozed off
In the woods,
Nestled in a small clearing
With the mist for a lover,

And dreamt I had
The stern eye
Of that bird
Watching me sleep.

Two Riddles

Hangs by a thread —
Whatever it is. Stripped naked.
Shivering. Human. Mortal.
On a thread finer than starlight.

By a power of a feeling,
Hangs, impossible, unthinkable,
Between the earth and the sky.
I, it says. I. I.

And how it boasts,
That everything that is to be known
About the wind
Is being revealed to it as it hangs.

∎

It goes without saying . . .
What does? No one knows.
Goes mysterious, ah funereal,
Goes for the hell of it.

If it has an opinion,
It keeps it to itself.
If it brings tidings,
It plays dumb, plays dead.

No use trying to pin it down.
It's elusive, of a retiring habit,
In a hurry of course, scurrying —
A blink of an eye and it's gone.

All that's known about it,
Is that it goes goes
Without saying.

Brooms

for Tomaz, Susan, and George

1

Only brooms
Know the devil
Still exists,

That the snow grows whiter
After a crow has flown over it,
That a dark dusty corner
Is the place of dreamers and children,

That a broom is also a tree
In the orchard of the poor,
That a hanging roach there
Is a mute dove.

2

Brooms appear in dream books
As omens of approaching death.
This is their secret life.
In public, they act like flat-chested old maids
Preaching temperance.

They are sworn enemies of lyric poetry.
In prison they accompany the jailer,
Enter cells to hear confessions.
Their short end comes down
When you least expect it.

Left alone behind a door
Of a condemned tenement,
They mutter to no one in particular,
Words like *virgin wind moon-eclipse*,
And that most sacred of all names:
Hieronymus Bosch.

3

In this and in no other manner
Was the first ancestral broom made:
Namely, they plucked all the arrows
From the bent back of Saint Sebastian.
They tied them with the rope
On which Judas hung himself.
Stuck in the stilt
On which Copernicus
Touched the morning star . . .

Then the broom was ready
To leave the monastery.
The dust welcomed it —
The old pornographer
Immediately wanted to
Peek under its skirt.

4

The secret teaching of brooms
Excludes optimism, the consolation
Of laziness, the astonishing wonders
Of a glass of aged moonshine.

It says: the bones end up under the table.
Bread crumbs have a mind of their own.
The milk is you-know-who's semen.
The mice have the last squeal.

As for the famous business
Of levitation, I suggest remembering:
There is only one God
And his prophet is Muhammed.

5

And then finally there's your grandmother
Sweeping the dust of the nineteenth century
Into the twentieth, and your grandfather plucking
A straw out of the broom to pick his teeth.

Long winter nights.
Dawns a thousand years deep.
Kitchen windows like heads
Bandaged for toothache.

The broom beyond them sweeping,
Tucking the lucent grains of dust
Into neat pyramids,
That have tombs in them,

Already sacked by robbers,
Once, long ago.

Watermelons

Green Buddhas
On the fruit stand.
We eat the smile
And spit out the teeth.

The Place

They were talking about the war,
The table still uncleared in front of them.
Across the way, the first window
Of the evening was already lit.
He sat, hunched over, quiet,
The old fear coming over him . . .
It grew darker. She got up to take the plate —
Now harshly white — to the kitchen.
Outside in the fields, in the woods,
A bird spoke in proverbs,
A Pope went out to meet Attila,
The ditch was ready for the firing squad.

Breasts

I love breasts, hard
Full breasts, guarded
By a button.

They come in the night.
The bestiaries of the ancients
Which include the unicorn
Have kept them out.

Pearly, like the east
An hour before sunrise,
Two ovens of the only
Philosopher's stone
Worth bothering about.

They bring on their nipples
Beads of inaudible sighs,
Vowels of delicious clarity
For the little red schoolhouse of our mouths.

Elsewhere, solitude
Makes another gloomy entry
In its ledger, misery
Borrows another cup of rice.

They draw nearer: Animal
Presence. In the barn
The milk shivers in the pail.

I like to come up to them
From underneath, like a kid
Who climbs on a chair
To reach a jar of forbidden jam.

Gently, with my lips,
Loosen the button.
Have them slip into my hands
Like two freshly poured beer mugs.

I spit on fools who fail to include
Breasts in their metaphysics,
Stargazers who have not enumerated them
Among the moons of the earth . . .

They give each finger
Its true shape, its joy:
Virgin soap, foam
On which our hands are cleansed.

And how the tongue honors
These two sour buns,
For the tongue is a feather
Dipped in egg yolk.

I insist that a girl
Stripped to the waist
Is the first and last miracle,
That the old janitor on his deathbed
Who demands to see the breasts of his wife
For one last time
Is the greatest poet who ever lived.

O my sweet yes, my sweet no,
Look, everyone is asleep on the earth.
Now, in the hush,
Drawing the waist
Of the one I love to mine,

I will tip each breast
Like a dark heavy grape
Into the hive
Of my drowsy mouth.

Charles Simic

Charles Simic is a sentence.
A sentence has a beginning and an end.

Is he a simple or compound sentence?
It depends on the weather,
It depends on the stars above.

What is the subject of the sentence?
The subject is your beloved Charles Simic.

How many verbs are there in the sentence?
Eating, sleeping, and fucking are some of its verbs.

What is the object of the sentence?
The object, my little ones,
Is not yet in sight.

And who is writing this awkward sentence?
A blackmailer, a girl in love,
And an applicant for a job.

Will they end with a period or a question mark?
They'll end with an exclamation point and an ink spot.

Solitude

There now, where the first crumb
Falls from the table
You think no one hears it
As it hits the floor,

But somewhere already
The ants are putting on
Their Quaker hats
And setting out to visit you.

The Chicken Without a Head

When two times two was three,
The chicken without a head was hatched.
When the earth was still flat,
It fell off its edge, daydreaming.
When there were 13 signs in the zodiac,
It found a dead star for its gizzard.
When the first fox was getting married,
It taught itself to fly with one wing.
When all the eggs were still golden,
The clouds in the sky tasted like sweet corn.
When the rain flooded its coop,
Its wishbone was its ark.
Ah, when the chicken had only itself to roast,
The lightning was its skewer,
The thunder its baste and salt.

The chicken without a head made a sigh,
And then a hailstone out of that sigh,
And the window for the hailstone to strike.
Nine lives it made for itself,
And nine coats of solitude to dress them in.
It made its own shadow. Not true.
It only made a flea to bite holes in the dark.
Made it all out of nothing. Made a needle
To sew back its broken eggshell.
Made the lovers naked. Everybody else put clothes on them.
Its father made the knife, but it polished the blade,
Until it threw back its image like a funhouse mirror.
Made it all out of raglets of time.
Who's to say it'd be happier if it didn't?

3

Hear the song of a chicken without a head
As it goes scratching in grave dirt.
A song in which two parallel lines
Meet at infinity, in which God
Makes the last of the little apples,
In which golden fleece is heard growing
On a sad girl's pubes. The song
Of swearwords dreaming of a pure mouth.
The song of a doornail raised from the dead.
The song in half whisper because accomplices
Have been found, because the egg's safe
In the cuckoo's nest. The song
You wade into until your own hat floats.
A song of contagious laughter.
A lethal song.
That's right, the song of dark premonitions.

4

On a headless evening of a headless day
The chicken on fire and the words
Around it like a ring of fabulous beasts.
Each night it threw them a bite-size portion of its heart.
The words were hungry, the night held the fork.
Whatever the gallows bird made, its head unmade,
Its long-lost, axed-off head
Rose into the sky in a balloon of question marks.
Down below the great banquet went on:
The table that supplies itself with bread.
A saw that cuts a dream in half.
Wings so quick they don't get wet in heavy rain.
The egg that mutters to the frying pan:
I swear it by the hair in my yolk,
There's no such thing as a chicken without a head.

5

The chicken without a head ran a maze,
Ran half-plucked,
A serving fork stuck in its back,
Ran, backward, into the blue of the evening.
Ran upside down,
Someone huge and red-aproned rose in its wake.
Ran leaving its squinting head far behind,
Its head with a shock of red hair.
Ran up the church steeple,
And up the lightning rod on that steeple
For the wind to ruffle its feathers.
Ran, and is still running this Good Friday,
Between raindrops,
Hellfoxes on its trail.

White

Out of poverty
To begin again

With the taste of silence
On my tongue

Say a word,
Then listen to it fray

Thread by thread,
In the fading,

The already vanishing
Evening light.

So clear, it's obscure
The sense of existing

In this very moment,
Cheek by jowl with

My shadow on the wall
With its long, gallowslike,

Contorted neck
Bloodied by the sunset,

Watching and listening
To my own heartbeat.

■

This is breath, only breath.
Think it over, friend.

A shit-house fly weighs
Twice as much.

But when I tell the world so,
I'm less by a breath.

The struck match flares up
And nods in agreement

Before the dark claps it
With its heavy hands.

■

As strange as a shepherd
In the Arctic Circle.

Someone like Bo-peep.
All her sheep are white

And she can't get any sleep
Over lost sheep,

So she plays a flute
Which cries Bo-peep,

Which says, poor girl,
Take care of your sheep.

■

On a late afternoon of snow,
In a small unlit grocery store

Where a door has just opened
With a long, painful squeak,

A small boy carries a piece of paper
Between his thumb and forefinger

To the squint-eyed old woman
Bending low over the counter.

It's that paper I'm remembering,
And the quiet and the shadows.

■

You're not what you seem to be.
I'm not what I seem to be.

It's as if we were the unknowing
Inmates of someone's shadow box,

And its curtain was our breath
And so were the images it caught,

Which were like the world we know.
His gloves as gray as the sky

While he held us up by our feet
Swaying over the earth to and fro.

■

We need a marrying preacher.
Some crow, praise be,

By the side of the road
With a bloody beak

Studying a wind-leafed
Black book

All of whose pages are gold-edged
And blank,

While we wait, with frost thickening
On our eyelashes.

■

The sky of the desert,
The heavens of the crucified.

The great white sky
Of the visionaries.

Its one lone, ghostlike
Buzzard still hovering,

Writing the long century's
Obituary column

Over the white city,
The city of our white nights.

■

Mother gives me to the morning
On the threshold.

I have the steam of my breath
For a bride.

The snow on my shoes
The hems of her wedding dress,

My love always a step ahead,
Always a blur,

A whiteout
In the raging, dreamlike storm.

■

As if I shut my eyes
In order to peek

At the world unobserved,
And saw

The nameless
In its glory.

And knew no way
To speak of it,

And did, nevertheless,
And then said something else.

■

What are you up to, smart-ass?
I turn on my tongue's skewer.

What do you baste yourself with?
I cough bile laced with blood.

Do you use pepper and salt?
I bite words as they come into my mouth.

And how will you know you're done?
My eyes will burn till I see clear.

What will you carve yourself with?
I'll let my tongue be the knife.

■

In the inky forest,
In its maziest,

Murkiest scribble
Of words

And wordless cries,
I went for a glimpse

Of the blossomlike
White erasure

Over a huge,
Furiously crossed-out something.

■

I can't say I'm much of a cook,
If my heart is in the fire with the onions.

I can't say I'm much of a hero,
If the weight of my head has me pinned down.

I can't say I'm in charge here,
If the flies hang their hats in my mouth.

I can't say I am the smart one,
If I wait for a star to answer me.

Nor can I call myself good-for-nothing.
Thanks to me the worms will have their dinner.

■

One has to make do.
Make ends meet,

Odds and ends.
Make no bones about it.

Make a stab in the dark.
Make the hair curl.

Make a door-to-nowhere.
Make a megaphone with one's hands,

And call and make do
With the silence answering.

■

Then all's well and white
All day and all night.

The highways are snowbound.
The forest paths are hushed.

The power lines have fallen.
The windows are dark.

Nothing but starlight
And the snow's dim light

And the wind wildly
Preaching in the pine tree.

■

In an unknown year
Of an evil-eyed century,

On a day of biting wind,
A tiny old woman,

One foot in the grave,
Met a boy playing hooky.

She offered him a sugar cube
In a hand so wizened

His tongue leapt back in fear
Saying thanks.

■

Do you take this line
Stretching to infinity?

I take this white paper
Lying still before me.

Do you take this ring
Of unknown circumference?

I take this breath
Slipping in and out of it.

Then you may kiss the place
Where your pencil went faint.

■

Had to get through me
On its long, long trek

To and from nowhere.
Woe to every heartbeat

That stood in its way,
Woe to every thought . . .

Time's white ants hurrying,
The rustle of their feet.

Gravedigger ants.
Village idiot ants.

∎

I haven't budged from the start.
Five fingers crumpled up

Over the blank page
As if composing a love letter,

Do you hear the white night
Touching down?

I hear its ear trumpets,
The holy escutcheons

Turning golden
In the dying light.

∎

Psst. The white hair
Fallen from my head

On the writing paper
Momentarily anonymous.

I had to bend down low
And put my eye next to it

To make sure,
Then nudge it, ever so slowly

With the long tip of my pencil
Over the edge of the table.

What the White Had to Say

Because I'm nothing you can name,
I knew you long before you knew me.
Some days you keep your hand closed
As if you've caught me,
But it's only a fly you've got there.
No use calling on angels and devils
In the middle of the night.
Go ahead, squint into the dregs on the bottom
Of your coffee cup, for all I care.
I do not answer to your hocus-pocus,
For I'm nearer to you than your own breath.
One sun shines on us both
Through the slit in your eyelids.
Your empty hand shows me off
To the four white walls of your room,

While with my horse's tail I wave the fly away,
But there's no tail, and the fly
Is a white thought buzzing in your head.

Because I'm nothing you'll ever name,
You sharpen your tongue hoping to skewer me.
The ear that rose in the night
To hear the truth inside the word *love*.
Listen to this, my beloved,
I'm the great nothing that tucked you in,
The finger placed softly on your lips
That made you sit up in bed wide awake.
Still, this riddle comes with no answer.
The same mother left us on your doorstep.
The same high ceiling made us insomniac.
Late-night piano picking out blue notes
In the empty ballroom down the hall,
We've fallen in the gaps between the notes.
And still you want me to say more?
Time has stopped. Your shadow,
With its gallowslike head and neck,
Has not stirred on the wall.

The Partial Explanation

Seems like a long time
Since the waiter took my order.
Grimy little luncheonette,
The snow falling outside.

Seems like it has grown darker
Since I last heard the kitchen door

Behind my back
Since I last noticed
Anyone pass on the street.

A glass of ice water
Keeps me company
At this table I chose myself
Upon entering.

And a longing,
Incredible longing
To eavesdrop
On the conversation
Of cooks.

The Lesson

It occurs to me now
that all these years
I have been
the idiot pupil
of a practical joker.

Diligently
and with foolish reverence
I wrote down
what I took to be
his wise pronouncements
concerning
my life on earth.
Like a parrot
I rattled off the dates
of wars and revolutions.

I rejoiced
at the death of my tormentors.
I even became convinced
that their number
was diminishing.

It seemed to me
that gradually
my teacher was revealing to me
a pattern,
that what I was being told
was an intricate plot
of a picaresque novel
in installments,
the last pages of which
would be given over
entirely
to lyrical evocations
of nature.

Unfortunately,
with time,
I began to detect in myself
an inability
to forget even
the most trivial detail.
I lingered more and more
over the beginnings:
The haircut of a soldier
who was urinating
against our fence;
shadows of trees on the ceiling,
the day
my mother and I

had nothing to eat . . .
Somehow,
I couldn't get past
that prison train
that kept waking me up
every night.
I couldn't get that whistle
that rumble
out of my head . . .

In this classroom
austerely furnished
by my insomnia,
at the desk consisting
of my two knees,
for the first time
in this long and terrifying
apprenticeship,
I burst out laughing.
Forgive me, all of you!
At the memory of my uncle
charging a barricade
with a homemade bomb,
I burst out laughing.

A Landscape with Crutches

So many crutches. Now even the daylight
Needs one, even the smoke
As it goes up. And the shacks—
One per customer—they move off
In a single file with difficulty,

I said, with a hell of an effort . . .
And the trees behind them about to stumble,
And the ants on their toy crutches,
And the wind on its ghost crutch.

I can't get any peace around here:
The bread on its artificial legs,
A headless doll in a wheelchair,
And my mother, mind you, using
Two knives for crutches as she squats to pee.

Help Wanted

They ask for a knife
I come running
They need a lamb
I introduce myself as the lamb

A thousand sincere apologies
It seems they require some rat poison
They require a shepherd
For their flock of black widows

Luckily I've brought my bloody
Letters of recommendation
I've brought my death certificate
Signed and notarized

But they've changed their minds again
Now they want a songbird, a bit of springtime
They want a woman
To soap and kiss their balls

It's one of my many talents
(I assure them)
Chirping and whistling like an aviary
Spreading the cheeks of my ass

Animal Acts

A bear who eats with a silver spoon.
Two apes adept at grave-digging.
Rats who do calculus.
A police dog who copulates with a woman,
Who takes undertaker's measurements.

A bedbug who suffers, who has doubts
About his existence. The miraculous
Laughing dove. A thousand-year-old turtle
Playing billiards. A chicken who
Cuts his own throat, who bleeds.

The trainer with his sugar cubes,
With his chair and whip. The evenings
When they all huddle in a cage,
Smoking cheap cigars, lazily
Marking the cards in the new deck.

Charon's Cosmology

With only his dim lantern
To tell him where he is
And every time a mountain
Of fresh corpses to load up

Take them to the other side
Where there are plenty more
I'd say by now he must be confused
As to which side is which

I'd say it doesn't matter
No one complains he's got
Their pockets to go through
In one a crust of bread in another a sausage

Once in a long while a mirror
Or a book which he throws
Overboard into the dark river
Swift and cold and deep

The Ballad of the Wheel

so that's what it's like to be a wheel
so that's what it's like to be tied to one of its spokes
while the rim screeches while the axle grinds
so that's what it's like to have the earth and heaven confused
to speak of the stars on the road
of stones churning in the icy sky
to suffer as the wheel suffers
to bear its unimaginable weight

if only it were a honing wheel
I would have its sparks to see by
if only it were a millstone
I would have bread to keep my mouth busy
if only it were a roulette wheel
my left eye would watch its right dance in it

so that's what it's like
to be chained to the wounded rib of a wheel
to move as the hearse moves
to move as the lumber truck moves
down the mountains at night

what do you think my love
while the wheel turns

I think of the horse out in front
how the snowflakes are caught in his mane
how he shakes his beautiful blindfolded head
I think how in the springtime
two birds are pulling us along as they fly
how one bird is a crow

and the other a swallow
I think how in the summertime
there's no one out there
except the clouds in the blue sky
except the dusk in the blue sky
I think how in autumn
there's a man harnessed out there
a bearded man with the bit stuck in his mouth
a hunchback with a blanket over his shoulders
hauling the wheel
heavy as the earth

don't you hear I say don't you hear
the wheel talks as it turns

I have the impression that it's hugging me closer
that it has maternal instincts
that it's telling me a bedtime story
that it knows the way home
that I grit my teeth just like my father

I have the impression
that it whispers to me
how all I have to do
to stop its turning
is to hold my breath

A Wall

That's the only image
That turns up.

A wall all by itself,
Poorly lit, beckoning,
But no sense of the room,
Not even a hint
Of why it is I remember
So little and so clearly:

The fly I was watching,
The details of its wings
Glowing like turquoise.
Its feet, to my amusement
Following a minute crack —
An eternity
Around that simple event.

And nothing else; and nowhere
To go back to;
And no one else
As far as I know to verify.

The Terms

A child crying in the night
Across the street
In one of the many dark windows.
That, too, to get used to,
Make part of your life.
Like this book of astronomy
Which you open with equal apprehension
By the light of table lamp,
And your birdlike shadow on the wall.
A sleepless witness at the base
Of this expanding immensity,
Simultaneous in this moment
With all of its empty spaces,
Listening to a child crying in the night
With a hope,
It will go on crying a little longer.

Eyes Fastened with Pins

How much death works,
No one knows what a long
Day he puts in. The little
Wife always alone
Ironing death's laundry.

The beautiful daughters
Setting death's supper table.
The neighbors playing
Pinochle in the backyard
Or just sitting on the steps
Drinking beer. Death,
Meanwhile, in a strange
Part of town looking for
Someone with a bad cough,
But the address is somehow wrong,
Even death can't figure it out
Among all the locked doors . . .
And the rain beginning to fall.
Long windy night ahead.
Death with not even a newspaper
To cover his head, not even
A dime to call the one pining away,
Undressing slowly, sleepily,
And stretching naked
On death's side of the bed.

The Prisoner

He is thinking of us.
These leaves, their lazy rustle
That made us sleepy after lunch
So we had to lie down.

He considers my hand on her breast,
Her closed eyelids, her moist lips
Against my forehead, and the shadows of trees
Hovering on the ceiling.

It's been so long. He has trouble
Deciding what else is there.
And all along the suspicion
That we do not exist.

Empire of Dreams

On the first page of my dreambook
It's always evening
In an occupied country.
Hour before the curfew.
A small provincial city.
The houses all dark.
The storefronts gutted.

I am on a street corner
Where I shouldn't be.
Alone and coatless
I have gone out to look
For a black dog who answers to my whistle.
I have a kind of Halloween mask
Which I am afraid to put on.

Prodigy

I grew up bent over
a chessboard.

I loved the word *endgame*.

All my cousins looked worried.

It was a small house
near a Roman graveyard.
Planes and tanks
shook its windowpanes.

A retired professor of astronomy
taught me how to play.

That must have been in 1944.

In the set we were using,
the paint had almost chipped off
the black pieces.

The white King was missing
and had to be substituted for.

I'm told but do not believe
that that summer I witnessed
men hung from telephone poles.

I remember my mother
blindfolding me a lot.
She had a way of tucking my head
suddenly under her overcoat.

In chess, too, the professor told me,
the masters play blindfolded,
the great ones on several boards
at the same time.

Baby Pictures of Famous Dictators

The epoch of a streetcar drawn by horses,
The organ-grinder and his monkey.
Women with parasols. Little kids in rowboats
Photographed against a cardboard backdrop depicting
    an idyllic sunset
At the fairgrounds where they all went to see
The two-headed calf, the bearded
Fat lady who dances the dance of seven veils.

And the great famine raging through India . . .
Fortunetelling white rat pulling a card out of a shoebox
While Edison worries over the lightbulb,
And the first model of the sewing machine
Is delivered in a pushcart
To a modest white-fenced home in the suburbs,

Where there are always a couple of infants
Posing for the camera in their sailors' suits,
Out there in the garden overgrown with shrubs.
Lovable little mugs smiling faintly toward
The new century. Innocent. Why not?
All of them like ragdolls of the period
With those chubby porcelain heads
That shut their long eyelashes as you lay them down.

In a kind of perpetual summer twilight . . .
One can even make out the shadow of the tripod and the
    black hood
That must have been quivering in the breeze.

One assumes that they all stayed up late squinting at the stars,
And were carried off to bed by their mothers and big sisters.
While the dogs remained behind:
Pedigreed bitches pregnant with bloodhounds.

Shirt

To get into it
As it lies
Crumpled on the floor
Without disturbing a single crease

Respectful
Of the way I threw it down
Last night
The way it happened to land

Almost managing
The impossible contortions
Doubling back now
Through a knotted sleeve

Begotten of the Spleen

The Virgin Mother walked barefoot
Among the land mines.
She carried an old man in her arms
Like a howling babe.

The earth was an old people's home.
Judas was the night nurse,
Emptying bedpans into the river Jordan,
Tying people on a dog chain.

The old man had two stumps for legs.
St. Peter came pushing a cart
Loaded with flying carpets.
They were not flying carpets.

They were piles of bloody diapers.
The Magi stood around
Cleaning their nails with bayonets.
The old man gave little Mary Magdalene

A broken piece of a mirror.
She hid in the church outhouse.
When she got thirsty she licked
The steam off the glass.

That leaves Joseph. Poor Joseph,
Standing naked in the snow.
He only had a rat
To load his suitcases on.

The rat wouldn't run into its hole.
Even when the searchlights came on
Up in the guard towers
And caught them standing there.

Toy Factory

My mother works here,
And so does my father.

It's the night shift.
At the assembly line,
They wind toys up
To inspect their springs.

The seven toy members
Of the firing squad
Point their rifles,
And lower them quickly.

The one being shot at
Falls and gets up,
Falls and gets up.
His blindfold is just painted on.

The toy gravediggers
Don't work so well.
Their spades are heavy,
Their spades are much too heavy.

Perhaps that's how
It's supposed to be?

The Little Tear Gland That Says

Then there was Johann,
the carousel horse —
except he wasn't really a carousel horse.

He grew up in "the naive realism of the Wolffian school
which without close scrutiny regards
logical necessity and reality as identical."

On Sundays, his parents took him
to the undertaker's for cookies.
"All these people flying in their dreams,"
he thought.

Standing before the Great Dark Night of History,
a picture of innocence
held together by his mother's safety pins,
short and bowlegged.

Cool reflection soon showed
there were openings among the signatories of
    death sentences . . .
plus free high leather boots that squeak.

On his entrance exam he wrote:
"The act of torture consists of various strategies
meant to increase the imagination
of the *Homo sapiens*."

And then . . . the Viennese waltz.

The Stream

for Russ Banks

The ear threading
the eye

all night long
the ear
on a long errand
for the eye

through the thickening
pine
white birch
over no-man's-land

pebbles
is it
compact in their anonymity
their gravity

accidents of location
abstract necessity

water
which takes such pains

to convince me
it is flowing

■

Summoning me
to be
two places at once

to drift
the length
of its chill
its ache

hand white
at the knuckles

live bait
the old hide-and-seek
in and out
of the swirl

luminous verb
carnivorous verb
innocent as sand
under its blows

■

An insomnia as big
as the stars'

always
on the brink —
as it were
of some deeper utterance

some harsher
reckoning

at daybreak
lightly
oh so lightly
when she brushes
against me

and the hems of her long skirt
go trailing

a bit longer

■

Nothing
that comes to nothing
for company

comes the way a hurt
the way a thought
comes

comes and keeps coming

all night meditating
on what she asks of me
when she doesn't

when I hear myself say
she doesn't

Furniture Mover

Ah the great
    the venerable
whoever he is

    ahead of me
huge load
    terrific backache

    wherever
a chair's waiting
    meadow
sky
    beckoning

he is the one
    that's been
there
    without instructions
and for no wages

a huge load
on his back
     and under his arm
thus
     always

     all in place
perfect
     just as it was
sweet home

     at the address
I never even dreamed of
     the address
I'm already changing

     in a hurry
to overtake him
     to arrive
not ahead

     but just as
he sets down
     the table
the thousand-year-old
     bread crumbs

     I used to
claim
     I was part
of his load

     high up there

roped safely
    with the junk
the eviction notices

    I used to
prophesy
    he'll stumble
by and by

    No luck—
oh
    Mr. Furniture Mover
on my knees

    let me come
for once
    early
to where it's vacant

    you still
on the stairs
    wheezing
between floors

and me behind the door
    in the gloom
I think I would
    let you do

what you must

Elegy

Note
as it gets darker
    that little
can be ascertained
of the particulars
    and of their true .
magnitudes

note
the increasing
    unreliability
of vision
though one thing may appear
    more or less
familiar
    than another

    disengaged
from reference
as they are
    in the deepening
gloom

    nothing to do
but sit
    and abide
depending on memory
to provide
    the vague outline
the theory
of where we are
tonight

and why
we can see
so little
    of each other
and soon
    will be
even less
    able

    in this starless
summer night
    windy and cold

    at the table
brought out
    hours ago
under a huge ash tree
    two chairs
two ambiguous figures
    each one relying
on the other
to remain faithful
    now
that one can leave
    without the other one
    knowing

    this late
in what only recently was
    a garden
a festive occasion
    elaborately planned
for two lovers

             in the open air
at the end
       of a dead-end
road
       rarely traveled

       o love

Note Slipped Under a Door

I saw a high window struck blind
By the late afternoon sunlight.

I saw a towel
With many dark fingerprints
Hanging in the kitchen.

I saw an old apple tree,
A shawl of wind over its shoulders,
Inch its lonely way
Toward the barren hills.

I saw an unmade bed
And felt the cold of its sheets.

I saw a fly soaked in pitch
Of the coming night
Watching me because it couldn't get out.

I saw stones that had come
From a great purple distance
Huddle around the front door.

Grocery

Figure or figures unknown
Keep a store
Keep it open
Nights and all day Sunday

Half of what they sell
Will kill you
The other half
Makes you go back for more

Too cheap to turn on the lights
Hard to tell what it is
They've got on the counter
What it is you're paying for

All the rigors
All the solemnities
Of a brass scale imperceptibly quivering
In the early winter dusk

One of its pans
For their innards
The other one for yours —
And yours heavier

Classic Ballroom Dances

Grandmothers who wring the necks
Of chickens; old nuns
With names like Theresa, Marianne,
Who pull schoolboys by the ear;

The intricate steps of pickpockets
Working the crowd of the curious
At the scene of an accident; the slow shuffle
Of the evangelist with a sandwich board;

The hesitation of the early-morning customer
Peeking through the window grille
Of a pawnshop; the weave of a little kid
Who is walking to school with eyes closed;

And the ancient lovers, cheek to cheek,
On the dance floor of the Union Hall,
Where they also hold charity raffles
On rainy Monday nights of an eternal November.

Progress Report

And how are the rats doing in the maze?
The gray one in a baggy fur coat
Appears dazed, the rest squeeze past him
Biting and squealing.

A pretty young attendant has him by the tail.
She is going to slit him open.
The blade glints and so do the beads
Of perspiration on her forehead.

His cousins are still running in circles.
The damp, foul-smelling sewer
Where they nuzzled their mother's teat
Is what they hope to see at the next turn.

Already she's yanked his heart out,
And he doesn't know what for?
Neither does she at this moment
Watching his eyes glaze, his whiskers twitch.

Winter Night

The church is an iceberg.

It's the wind. It must be blowing tonight
Out of those galactic orchards,
Their Copernican pits and stones.

The monster created by the mad Dr. Frankenstein
Sailed for the New World,
And ended up some place like New Hampshire.

Actually, it's just a local drunk,
Knocking with a snow shovel,
Wanting to go in and warm himself.

An iceberg, the book says, is a large drifting
Piece of ice, broken off a glacier.

The Cold

As if in a presence of an intelligence
Concentrating. I thought myself
Scrutinized and measured closely
By the sky and the earth,

And then algebraized and entered
In a notebook page blank and white,
Except for the faint blue lines
Which might have been bars,

For I kept walking and walking,
And it got darker and then there was
A flicker of a light or two
Far above and beyond my cage.

Devotions

for Michael Anania

The hundred-year-old servants
Are polishing the family silver,
And recalling the little master dressed as a girl
Peeing in a chamber pot.

Now he is away hunting with Madame.
The reverend dropped by this afternoon
And inquired amiably after them.
His pink fingers were like squirming piglets.

Even the Siamese cats like to sit and gaze,
On days when it rains and the fire is lit,
At the grandfather with waxed mustache-tips
Scowling out of the heavy picture frame.

They were quick to learn respect
And what is expected of them, these former
Farm boys and girls stealing glances
At themselves in spoons large and small.

Cold Blue Tinge

The pink-cheeked Jesus
Thumbtacked above
The cold gas stove,
And the boy sitting on the piss pot
Blowing soap bubbles
For the black kitten to catch.

Very peaceful, except
There's a faint moan
From the next room.
His mother's asking
For some more pills,
But there's no reply.
The bubbles are quiet,
And kitten is sleepy.

All his brothers and sisters
Have been drowned.
He'll have a long life, though,
Catching mice for the baker,
And the undertaker.

The Writings of the Mystics

On the counter among many
Much-used books,
The rare one you must own
Immediately, the one
That makes your heart race

As you wait for small change
With a silly grin
You'll take to the street,
And later, past the landlady
Watching you wipe your shoes,

Then, up to the rented room
Which neighbors the one
Of a nightclub waitress
Who's shaving her legs
With a door partly open,

While you turn to the first page
Which speaks of a presentiment
Of a higher existence
In things familiar and drab . . .

In a house soon to be torn down,
Suddenly hushed, and otherworldly . . .
You have to whisper your own name,
And the words of the hermit,

Since it must be long past dinner,
The one they ate quickly,
Happy that your small portion
Went to the three-legged dog.

Window Washer

And again the screech of the scaffold
High up there where all our thoughts converge:
Lightheaded, hung
By a leather strap,

Twenty stories up
In the chill of late November
Wiping the grime
Off the pane, the many windows

Which have no way of opening,
Tinted windows mirroring the clouds
That are like equestrian statues,
Phantom liberators with sabers raised

Before these dark offices,
And their anonymous multitudes
Bent over this day's
Wondrously useless labor.

Gallows Etiquette

Our sainted great-great-
Grandmothers
Used to sit and knit
Under the gallows.

No one remembers what it was
They were knitting
And what happened when the ball of yarn
Rolled out of their laps
And had to be retrieved.

One pictures the hooded executioner
And his pasty-faced victim
Interrupting their grim business
To come quickly to their aid.

Confirmed pessimists
And other party poopers
Categorically reject
Such far-fetched notions
Of gallows etiquette.

In Midsummer Quiet

Ariadne's bird,
That lone
Whippoorwill.

Ball of twilight thread
Unraveling furtively.
Tawny thread,
Raw, pink the thread end.

A claw or two also
To pare, snip . . .
After which it sits still
For the stream to explain why it shivers

So.
  Resuming, farther on,
Intermittently,
By the barn
Where the first stars are —
In quotation marks,
As it were — O phantom

Bird!
Dreaming of my own puzzles
And mazes.

Peaceful Trees

in memory of M. N.

All shivers,
Dear friends.

Is it for me
You keep still?

Not a rustle
To remind me—

Quietly, the healing
Spreads—

A deep shade
Over each face.

■

So many leaves,
And not one
Lately stirring.

So many already
Tongue-shaped,
Tip-of-the-tongue-shaped.

Oh the sweet speech of trees
In the evening breeze
Of some other summer.
Speech like sudden

Rustle of raindrops
Out of the high, pitch-blue
Heavens.

Lofty ones,
Do you shudder
When the chain saw
Cuts one of you?

Would it soothe,
If for all you voiceless,
To high heavens
The one with the rope round his neck

Were to plead?

■

Forgive me,

For the conjecture
I'm prone to —

Restless as I am
Before you windless,

Whispering
To the Master Whisperers

Of their own
Early-evening silences.

My Beloved

after D. Khrams

In the fine print of her face
Her eyes are two loopholes.
No, let me start again.
Her eyes are flies in milk,
Her eyes are baby Draculas.

To hell with her eyes.
Let me tell you about her mouth.
Her mouth's the red cottage
Where the wolf ate grandma.

Ah, forget about her mouth,
Let me talk about her breasts.
I get a peek at them now and then
And even that's more than enough
To make me lose my head,
So I better tell you about her legs.

When she crosses them on the sofa
It's like the jailer unwrapping a parcel
And in that parcel is a Christmas cake
And in that cake a sweet little file
That gasps her name as it files my chains.

Hurricane Season

Just as the world was ending
We fell in love,
Immoderately. I had a pair of

Blue pinstripe trousers
Impeccably pressed
Against misfortune;

You had a pair of silver,
Spiked-heeled shoes,
And a peekaboo blouse.

We looked swank kissing
While reflected in a pawnshop window:
Banjos and fiddles around us,

Even a gleaming tuba. I said,
Two phosphorescent minute hands
Against the Unmeasurables,

Geniuses when it came to
Undressing each other
By slow tantalizing degrees . . .

That happened in a crepuscular hotel
That had seen better days,
Across from some sort of august state institution,

Rain-blurred
With its couple of fake
Egyptian stone lions.

Note

A rat came on stage
During the performance
Of the school Christmas play.
Mary let out a scream
And dropped the infant
On Joseph's foot.
The three Magi remained
Frozen
In their colorful robes.
You could hear a pin drop
As the rat surveyed the manger
Momentarily
Before proceeding to the wings
Where someone hit him,
In earnest,
Once, and then twice more,
With a heavy object.

History

On a gray evening
Of a gray century,
I ate an apple
While no one was looking.

A small, sour apple
The color of wood fire
Which I first wiped
On my sleeve.

Then I stretched my legs
As far as they'd go,
Said to myself
Why not close my eyes now

Before the late
World News and Weather.

Strictly Bucolic

for Mark and Jules

Are these mellifluous sheep,
And these the meadows made twice melliferous by their
　　bleating?
Is that the famous mechanical windup shepherd
Who comes with instructions and service manual?

This must be the regulation white fleece
Bleached and starched to perfection,
And we could be posing for our first communion pictures,
Except for the nasty horns.

I am beginning to think this might be
The Angelic Breeders Association's
Millennial Company Picnic (all expenses paid)
With a few large black dogs as special guests.

These dogs serve as ushers and usherettes.
They're always studying the rules,
The exigencies of proper deportment
When they're not reading Theocritus,

Or wagging their tails at the approach of
Theodora. Or is it Theodosius? Or even Theodoric?
They're theomorfic, of course. They theologize.
Theogony is their favorite. They also love theomachy.

Now they hand out the blue ribbons.
Ah, there's one for everyone!
Plus the cauldrons of stinking cabbage and boiled turnips
Which don't figure in this idyll.

Crows

Just so that each stark,
Spiked twig,
May be even more fierce
With significance,

There are these birds
As further harbingers
Of the coming wintry reduction
To sign and enigma:

The impatient way
In which they shook snow
Off their wings,
And then remained, inexplicably

Thus, wings half-open,
Making two large algebraic X's
As if for emphasis,
Or in the mockery of . . .

February

The one who lights the wood stove
Gets up in the dark.

How cold the iron is to the hand
Groping to open the flue,
The hand that will draw back
At the roar of the wind outside.

The wood that no longer smells of the woods;
The wood that smells of rats and mice —
And the matches that are always so loud
In the glacial stillness.

By its flare you'll see her squat;
Gaunt, wide-eyed;
Her lips saying the stark headlines
Going up in flames.

Punch Minus Judy

Where the elevated subway slows down,
A row of broken windows,
Only a single one still intact
Open and thickly curtained.

That's where I once saw a thin arm
Slip out between the slits,
The hand open to feel for drops of rain,
Or to give us a papal blessing.

Another time, there were two—
Chopped off at the elbows
Raising a small, naked baby
For a breath of evening air

Above the sweltering street
With a gang of men partying
Out of brown paper bags,
One limping off, seemingly, in a huff.

Austerities

From the heel
Of a half-loaf
Of black bread,
They made a child's head.

Child, they said,
We've nothing for eyes,
Nothing to spare for ears
And nose.

Just a knife
To make a slit
Where your mouth
Ought to be.

You can grin,
You can eat,
Spit the crumbs
Into our faces.

Eastern European Cooking

While Marquis de Sade had himself buggered—
Oh just around the time the Turks
Were roasting my ancestors on spits,
Goethe wrote *The Sorrows of Young Werther*.

It was chilly, raw, down-in-the-mouth
We were slurping bean soup thick with smoked sausage,
On Second Avenue, where years before I saw an old horse
Pull a wagon piled up high with flophouse mattresses.

Anyway, as I was telling my uncle Boris,
With my mouth full of pig's feet and wine:
"While they were holding hands and sighing under parasols,
We were being hung by our tongues."

"I make no distinction between scum,"
He said, and he meant everybody,
Us and them: A breed of murderers' helpers,
Evil-smelling torturers' apprentices.

Which called for another bottle of Hungarian wine,
And some dumplings stuffed with prunes,
Which we devoured in silence
While the Turks went on beating their cymbals and drums.

Luckily we had this Transylvanian waiter,
A defrocked priest, ex–dancing school instructor,
Regarding whose excellence we were in complete agreement
Since he didn't forget the toothpicks with our bill.

My Weariness of Epic Proportions

I like it when
Achilles
Gets killed
And even his buddy Patroclus—
And that hothead Hector—
And the whole Greek and Trojan
Jeunesse dorée
Are more or less
Expertly slaughtered
So there's finally
Peace and quiet
(The gods having momentarily
Shut up)
One can hear
A bird sing
And a daughter ask her mother
Whether she can go to the well
And of course she can
By that lovely little path
That winds through
The olive orchard

Madonnas Touched Up with Goatees

Most ancient Metaphysics (poor Metaphysics!),
All decked out in imitation jewelry.
We went for a stroll, arm in arm, smooching in public
Despite the difference in ages.

It's still the nineteenth century, she whispered.
We were in a knife-fighting neighborhood
Among some rundown relics of the Industrial Revolution.
Just a little farther, she assured me,
In the back of a certain candy store only she knew about,
The customers were engrossed in the *Phenomenology of
    the Spirit.*

It's long past midnight, my dove, my angel!
We'd better be careful, I thought.
There were young hoods on street corners
With crosses and iron studs on their leather jackets.
They all looked like they'd read Darwin and that
    madman Pavlov,
And were about to ask us for a light.

Midpoint

No sooner had I left A.
Than I started doubting its existence:
Its streets and noisy crowds;
Its famous all-night cafés and prisons.

It was dinnertime. The bakeries were closing:
Their shelves empty and white with flour.
The grocers were lowering their iron grilles.
A lovely young woman was buying the last casaba melon.

Even the back alley where I was born
Blurs, dims . . . O rooftops!
Armadas of bedsheets and shirts
In the blustery, crimson dusk . . .

B. at which I am destined
To arrive by and by
Doesn't exist now. Hurriedly
They're building it for my arrival,

And on that day it will be ready:
Its streets and noisy crowds . . .
Even the schoolhouse where I first
Forged my father's signature . . .

Knowing that on the day
Of my departure
It will vanish forever
Just as A. did.

||

from Unending Blues

December

It snows
and still the derelicts
go
carrying sandwich boards —

one proclaiming
the end of the world
the other
the rates of a local barbershop

Toward Nightfall

for Don and Jane

The weight of tragic events
On everyone's back,
Just as tragedy
In the proper Greek sense
Was thought impossible
To compose in our day.

There were scaffolds,
Makeshift stages,
Puny figures on them,
Like small indistinct animals
Caught in the headlights
Crossing the road way ahead,

In the gray twilight
That went on hesitating

On the verge of a huge
Starless autumn night.
One could've been in
The back of an open truck
Hunkering because of
The speed and chill.

One could've been walking
With a sidelong glance
At the many troubling shapes
The bare trees made—
Like those about to shriek,
But finding themselves unable
To utter a word now.

One could've been in
One of these dying mill towns
Inside a small dim grocery
When the news broke.
One would've drawn near the radio
With the one many months pregnant
Who serves there at that hour.

Was there a smell of
Spilled blood in the air,
Or was it that other,
Much finer scent—of fear,
The fear of approaching death
One met on the empty street?

Monsters on movie posters, too,
Prominently displayed.
Then, six factory girls,

Arm in arm, laughing
As if they've been drinking.
At the very least, one
Could've been one of them.

The one with a mouth
Painted bright red,
Who feels out of sorts,
For no reason, very pale,
And so, excusing herself,
Vanishes where it says
Rooms for Rent,
And immediately goes to bed,
Fully dressed, only

To lie with eyes open,
Trembling, despite the covers.
It's just a bad chill,
She keeps telling herself
Not having seen the papers
Which the landlord has the dog
Bring from the front porch.

The old man never learned
To read well, and so
Reads on in that half-whisper,
And in that half-light
Verging on the dark,
About that day's tragedies
Which supposedly are not
Tragedies in the absence of
Figures endowed with
Classic nobility of soul.

Early Evening Algebra

The madwoman went marking X's
With a piece of school chalk
On the backs of unsuspecting
Hand-holding, homebound couples.

It was winter. It was dark already.
One could not see her face
Bundled up as she was and furtive.
She went as if windswept, as if crow-winged.

The chalk must have been given to her by a child.
One kept looking for him in the crowd,
Expecting him to be very pale, very serious,
Carrying a book or two in his hand.

Ever So Tragic

Heart — as in Latin pop songs
Blaring from the pool hall radio.
The air had thickened, the evening air.
He took off his white shirt.
The heart, one could mark it
With lipstick on a bare chest,
The way firing-squad commanders mark it.

He was reading in the papers
About the artificial heart.
The same plastic they use for wind-up toys,
She thought. More likely
Like an old wheelbarrow to push:

Heart of stone, knife grinder's
Stone . . .
                    Later
It was raining and they got into bed.
O desire, O futile hope, O sighs!
In coal miner's pit and lantern:
The heart, the bright red heart . . .

Didn't the blind man just call
His little dog that?

Hearts make haste, hasten on!

For the Sake of Amelia

Tending a cliff-hanging Grand Hotel
In a country ravaged by civil war.
My heart as its only bellhop.
My brain as its Chinese cook.

It's a rundown seaside place
With a row of gutted limousines out front,
Monkeys and fighting cocks in the great ballroom,
Potted palm trees grown wild to the ceilings.

Amelia surrounded by her beaus and fortunetellers,
Painting her eyelashes and lips blue
In the hour of dusk with the open sea beyond,
The long empty beaches, the tide's shimmer . . .

She pleading with me to check the ledgers,
Find out if Lenin stayed here once,
Buster Keaton, Nathaniel Hawthorne,
St. Bernard of Clairvaux, who wrote on love?

A hotel in which one tangos to a silence
Dark as cypresses in silent films . . .
In which children confide to imaginary friends . . .
In which pages of an important letter are flying . . .

But now a buzz from the suite with mirrors.
Amelia in the nude, black cotton over her eyes.
It seems there's a fly
Pestering her lover's Roman nose.

Night of distant guns, muffled and comfortable.
I am running with a flyswatter on a silver tray
Strewn with Turkish delights
And the Mask of Tragedy to cover her pubic hair.

At the Night Court

You've combed yourself carefully,
Your Honor, with a small fine-tooth comb
You then cleverly concealed
Before making your entrance
In the splendor of your black robes.

The comb tucked inside a handkerchief
Scented with the extract of dead roses —
While you took your high seat
Sternly eyeing each of the accused
In the hush of the empty courtroom.

The dark curly hairs in the comb
Did not come from your graying head.
One of the cleaning women used it on herself

While you dozed off in your chambers
Half undressed because of the heat.

The black comb in the pocket over the heart,
You feel it tremble just as ours do
When they ready themselves to make music
Lacking only the paper you're signing,
By the looks of it, with eyes closed.

Dark Farmhouses

Windy evening,
China-blue snow,
The old people are shivering
In their kitchens.

Truck without lights
Idling on the highway,
Is it a driver you require?
Wait a bit.

There's coal to load up,
A widow's sack of coal.

Is it a shovel you need?
Idle on,
A shovel will come by and by
Over the darkening plain.

A shovel,
And a spade.

Popular Mechanics

The enormous engineering problems
You'll encounter attempting to crucify yourself
Without helpers, pulleys, cogwheels,
And other clever mechanical contrivances—

In a small, bare, white room,
With only a loose-legged chair
To reach the height of the ceiling—
Only a shoe to beat the nails in.

Not to mention being naked for the occasion—
So that each rib and muscle shows.
Your left hand already spiked in,
Only the right to wipe the sweat with,

To help yourself to a butt
From the overflowed ashtray,
You won't quite manage to light—
And the night coming, the clever night.

The Fly

He was writing the History of Optimism
In Time of Madness. It was raining.
One of the local butcher's largest
Carrion fanciers kept pestering him.

There was a cat too watching the fly,
And a gouty-footed old woman
In a dirty bathrobe and frayed slippers
Bringing in a cup of pale tea.

With many sighs and long pauses
He found a bit of blue sky on the day of the Massacre of
    the Innocents.
He found a couple of lovers,
A meadow strewn with yellow flowers . . .

But he couldn't go on . . . O blue-winged, shivering one,
    he whispered.
Some days it's like using a white cane
And seeing mostly shadows
As one gropes for the words that come next!

Outside a Dirtroad Trailer

O exegetes, somber hermeneuts,
Ingenious untanglers of ambiguities,
A bald little man was washing
The dainty feet of a very fat woman.

In a chair under a soaring shade tree,
She kept giggling and shaking her huge breasts.
There was also a boy with glasses
Engrossed in a book of serious appearance.

One black sock drying on the line,
A parked hearse with trash cans in the back,
And a large flag hanging limp from the pole
On a day as yet unproclaimed as a holiday.

Dear Helen

There's a thing in the world
Called a sea cucumber.
I know nothing about it.
It just sounds cold and salty.
I think a salad of such cukes
Would be fine today.
I would have to dive for it, though,
Deep into the treacherous depths
While you mince the garlic
And sip the white wine
Into which the night is falling.
I should be back soon
With those lovely green vegetables
Out of the shark-infested sea.

Trees in the Open Country

for Jim

Like those who were eyewitnesses
to an enormity
And have since remained downcast
At the very spot,

Their shadows gradually lengthening
Into what look like canes, badly charred,
No choice but to lean on them eventually,
Together, and in a kind of reverie,

Awaiting the first solitary quip
From the maddeningly occulted birds,
Night birds bestirring themselves at last—
If you are still listening,

One has the impression the world
Is adamant on a matter of great importance,
And then—it isn't anymore . . .
Unless it's now the leaves' turn to reply?

October Arriving

I only have a measly ant
To think with today.
Others have pictures of saints,
Others have clouds in the sky.

The winter might be at the door,
For he's all alone
And in a hurry to hide.
Nevertheless, unable to decide

He retraces his steps
Several times and finds himself
On a huge blank wall
That has no window.

Dark masses of trees
Cast their mazes before him,
Only to erase them next
With a sly, sea-surging sound.

Ancient Autumn

Is that foolish youth still sawing
The good branch he's sitting on?
Do the hills wheeze like old men
And the few remaining apples sway?
Can he see the village in the valley
The way a chicken hawk would?

Already smoke rises over the roofs,
The days are getting short and chilly.
Even he must rest from time to time,
So he's lit a long-stemmed pipe
To watch a chimneysweep at work
And a woman pin diapers on the line
And then step behind some bushes,
Hike her skirt so her bare ass shows
While on the common humpbacked men
Roll a barrel of hard cider or beer,
And still beyond, past grazing cattle,
Children play soldier and march in step.

He thinks, if the wind changes direction,
He'll hear them shouting commands,
But it doesn't, so the black horseman
On the cobbled road remains inaudible.
One instant he's coming his way,
In the next he appears to be leaving in a hurry . . .
It's such scenes with their air of menace,
That make him muddled in the head.
He's not even aware that he has resumed sawing,
That the big red sun is about to set.

Against Whatever It Is That's Encroaching

Best of all is to be idle,
And especially on a Thursday,
And to sip wine while studying the light:
The way it ages, yellows, turns ashen
And then hesitates forever
On the threshold of the night
That could be bringing the first frost.

It's good to have a woman around just then,
And two is even better.
Let them whisper to each other
And eye you with a smirk.
Let them roll up their sleeves and unbutton their shirts a bit
As this fine old twilight deserves,

And the small schoolboy
Who has come home to a room almost dark
And now watches wide-eyed
The grownups raise their glasses to him,
The giddy-headed, red-haired woman
With eyes tightly shut,
As if she were about to cry or sing.

First Frost

The time of the year for the mystics.
October sky and the Cloud of Unknowing.
The routes of eternity beckoning.
Sign and enigma in the humblest of things.

Master cobbler Jakob Boehme
Sat in our kitchen all morning.
He sipped tea and warned of the quiet
To which the wise must school themselves.

The young woman paid no attention.
Hair fallen over her eyes,
Breasts loose and damp in her robe,
Stubbornly scrubbing a difficult stain.

Then the dog's bark brought us all outdoors,
And that wasn't just geese honking,
But Dame Julian of Norwich herself discoursing
On the marvelous courtesy and homeliness of the Maker.

Without a Sough of Wind

Against the backdrop
Of a twilight world
In which one has done so little
For one's soul

She hangs a skirt
On the doorknob
Puts a foot on the chair
To take off a black stocking

And it's good to have eyes
Just then for the familiar
Large swinging breasts
And the cleft of her ass

Before the recital
Of that long day's
Woes and forebodings
In the warm evening

With the drone of insects
On the window screen
And the lit dial of a radio
Providing what light there is

Its sound turned much too low
To make out the words
Of what sounds like
A silly old love song

| | |

from The World Doesn't End

My mother was a braid of black smoke.

She bore me swaddled over the burning cities.

The sky was a vast and windy place for a child to play.

We met many others who were just like us. They were trying to put on their overcoats with arms made of smoke.

The high heavens were full of little shrunken deaf ears instead of stars.

I was stolen by the gypsies. My parents stole me right back. Then the gypsies stole me again. This went on for some time. One minute I was in the caravan suckling the dark teat of my new mother, the next I sat at the long dining room table eating my breakfast with a silver spoon.

It was the first day of spring. One of my fathers was singing in the bathtub; the other one was painting a live sparrow the colors of a tropical bird.

She's pressing me gently with a hot steam iron, or she slips her hand inside me as if I were a sock that needed mending. The thread she uses is like the trickle of my blood, but the needle's sharpness is all her own.

"You will ruin your eyes, Henrietta, in such bad light," her mother warns. And she's right! Never since the beginning of the world has there been so little light. Our winter afternoons have been known at times to last a hundred years.

We were so poor I had to take the place of the bait in the mousetrap. All alone in the cellar, I could hear them pacing upstairs, tossing and turning in their beds. "These are dark and evil days," the mouse told me as he nibbled my ear. Years passed. My mother wore a cat-fur collar which she stroked until its sparks lit up the cellar.

I am the last Napoleonic soldier. It's almost two hundred years later and I am still retreating from Moscow. The road is lined with white birch trees and the mud comes up to my knees. The one-eyed woman wants to sell me a chicken, and I don't even have any clothes on.

The Germans are going one way; I am going the other. The Russians are going still another way and waving goodbye. I have a ceremonial saber. I use it to cut my hair, which is four feet long.

"Everybody knows the story about me and Dr. Freud," says my grandfather.

"We were in love with the same pair of black shoes in the window of the same shoe store. The store, unfortunately, was always closed. There'd be a sign: DEATH IN THE FAMILY or BACK AFTER LUNCH, but no matter how long I waited, no one would come to open.

"Once I caught Dr. Freud there shamelessly admiring the shoes. We glared at each other before going our separate ways, never to meet again."

He held the Beast of the Apocalypse by its tail! Oh beards on fire, our doom appeared sealed. The buildings were tottering; the computer screens were as dark as our grandmother's cupboard. We were too frightened to plead. Another century gone to hell—and for what? All because some people don't know how to bring up their children.

It was the epoch of the masters of levitation. Some evenings we saw solitary men and women floating above the dark tree-tops. Could they have been sleeping or thinking? They made no attempt to navigate. The wind nudged them ever so slightly. We were afraid to speak, to breathe. Even the nightbirds were quiet. Later, we'd mention the little book clasped in the hands of the young woman, and the way that old man lost his hat to the cypresses.

In the morning there were not even clouds in the sky. We saw a few crows preen themselves at the edge of the road; the shirts raise their empty sleeves on the blind woman's clothesline.

Ghost stories written as algebraic equations. Little Emily at the blackboard is very frightened. The X's look like a graveyard at night. The teacher wants her to poke among them with a piece of chalk. All the children hold their breath. The white chalk squeaks once among the plus and minus signs, and then it's quiet again.

The city had fallen. We came to the window of a house drawn by a madman. The setting sun shone on a few abandoned machines of futility. "I remember," someone said, "how in ancient times one could turn a wolf into a human and then lecture it to one's heart's content."

The stone is a mirror which works poorly. Nothing in it but dimness. Your dimness or its dimness, who's to say? In the hush your heart sounds like a black cricket.

Lover of endless disappointments with your collection of old postcards, I'm coming! I'm coming! You want to show me a train station with its clock stopped at five past five. We can't see inside the stationmaster's window because of the grime. We don't even know if there's a train waiting on the platform, much less if a woman in black is hurrying through the front door. There are no other people in sight, so it must be a quiet station. Some small town so effaced by time it has only one veiled widow left, and now she too is leaving with her secret.

The hundred-year-old china doll's head the sea washes up on its gray beach. One would like to know the story. One would like to make it up, make up many stories. It's been so long in the sea, the eyes and nose have been erased, its faint smile is even fainter. With the night coming, one would like to see one-self walking the empty beach and bending down to it.

Margaret was copying a recipe for "saints sautéed in onions" from an old cookbook. The ten thousand sounds of the world were hushed so we could hear the scratching of her pen. The saint was asleep in her bedroom with a wet cloth over his eyes. Outside the window, the author of the book sat in a flowering apple tree killing lice between his fingernails.

A poem about sitting on a New York rooftop on a chill autumn evening, drinking red wine, surrounded by tall buildings, the little kids running dangerously to the edge, the beautiful girl everyone's secretly in love with sitting by herself. She will die young but we don't know that yet. She has a hole in her black stocking, big toe showing, toe painted red . . . And the sky-scrapers . . . in the failing light . . . like new Chaldeans, pythonesses, Cassandras . . . because of their many blind windows.

"Tropical luxuriance around the idea of the soul," writes Nietzsche. I always felt that too, Friedrich! The Amazon jungle with its brightly colored birds squawking in every tree, but its depths dark and hushed. The beautiful lost girl is giving suck to a little monkey. The great lizard in attendance wears ecclesiastical robes and speaks French to her: "La Reine des Reines," he chants. Not the least charm of this tableau is that it can be so easily dismissed as preposterous and insulting to religious sentiments.

Are Russian cannibals worse than the English? Of course. The English eat only your heart, the Russians the soul. "The soul is a mirage in the desert," I told Anna Alexandrovna, but she went on eating mine anyway.

"Like a confit of duck, or like a sparkling littleneck clam still in its native brine?" I inquired. But she just rubbed her tummy and smiled naughtily at me from across the table.

My guardian angel is afraid of the dark. He pretends he's not, sends me ahead, tells me he'll be along in a moment. Pretty soon I can't see a thing. "This must be the darkest corner of heaven," someone whispers behind my back. It turns out her guardian angel is missing too. "It's an outrage," I tell her. "The dirty little cowards leaving us like this alone." And of course, for all we know, one of us may be an old man on his deathbed and the other one a sleepy little girl with glasses.

The old farmer in overalls hanging from a barn beam. The cows looking sideways. The old woman kneeling under his swaying feet in her Sunday black dress and touching the ground with her forehead like a Mohammedan. Outside the sky is full of sudsy clouds above an endless plowed field with no other land-marks in view.

O witches, O poverty! The two who with a sidelong glance measured the thinness of my neck through the bars of the bird-cage I carried on my shoulder . . .

They were far too young and elegant to be storybook witches. They wore low-cut party dresses, black seams in their stockings, lips thickly painted red.

The big-hearted trees offered their leaves by whispering armfuls over the winding path where the two eventually vanished.

I was left with my cage, its idiotic feeding dish, the even more absurd vanity mirror, and the faintly sounding silver bell.

Once I knew, then I forgot. It was as if I had fallen asleep in a field only to discover at waking that a grove of trees had grown up around me.

"Doubt nothing, believe everything" was my friend's idea of metaphysics, although his brother ran away with his wife. He still bought her a rose every day, sat in the empty house for the next twenty years talking to her about the weather.

I was already dozing off in the shade, dreaming that the rustling trees were my many selves explaining themselves all at the same time so that I could not make out a single word. My life was a beautiful mystery on the verge of understanding, always on the verge! Think of it!

My friend's empty house with every one of its windows lit. The dark trees multiplying all around it.

Thousands of old men with pants lowered sleeping in public restrooms. You're raving! You're exaggerating! Thousands of Maria Magdalenas, I see, kneeling at their feet, weeping.

A century of gathering clouds. Ghost ships arriving and leaving. The sea deeper, vaster. The parrot in the bamboo cage spoke several languages. The captain in the daguerreotype had his cheeks painted red. He brought a half-naked girl home from the tropics whom they kept chained in the attic till her death. After lunch, someone told of a race of people without mouths who subsisted only on the scent of flowers. It was the age of busy widow's walks, fires lit with pages of love letters, long-trailing white gowns and much soundless screaming in the small hours of the night.

The time of minor poets is coming. Goodbye Whitman, Dickinson, Frost. Welcome you whose fame will never reach beyond your closest family, and perhaps one or two good friends gathered after dinner over a jug of fierce red wine . . . while the children are falling asleep and complaining about the noise you're making as you rummage through the closets for your old poems, afraid your wife might've thrown them out with last spring's cleaning.

It's snowing, says someone who has peeked into the dark night, and then he, too, turns toward you as you prepare yourself to read, in a manner somewhat theatrical and with a face turning red, the long rambling love poem whose final stanza (unknown to you) is hopelessly missing.

—*after Aleksandar Ristović*

Lots of people around here have been taken for rides in UFOs. You wouldn't think that possible with all the pretty white churches in sight so well attended on Sundays.

"The round square doesn't exist," says the teacher to the dull-witted boy. His mother was abducted only last night. All expectations to the contrary, she sits in the corner grinning to herself. The sky is vast and blue.

"They're so small, they can sleep inside their own ears," says one eighty-year-old twin to the other.

My father loved the strange books of André Breton. He'd raise the wine glass and toast those far-off evenings "when butterflies formed a single uncut ribbon." Or we'd go out for a piss in the back alley and he'd say, "Here are some binoculars for blindfolded eyes." We lived in a rundown tenement that smelled of old people and their pets.

"Hovering on the edge of the abyss, permeated with the perfume of the forbidden," we'd take turns cutting the smoked sausage on the table. "I love America," he'd tell us. We were going to make a million dollars manufacturing objects we had seen in dreams that night.

Someone shuffles by my door muttering, "Our goose is cooked."

Strange! I have my knife and fork ready. I even have the napkin tied around my neck, but the plate before me is still empty.

Nevertheless, someone continues to mutter outside my door regarding a certain hypothetical, allegedly cooked goose that he claims is ours in common.

My Secret Identity Is

The room is empty,
And the window is open

IV

from The Book of Gods and Devils

The Little Pins of Memory

There was a child's Sunday suit
Pinned to a tailor's dummy
In a dusty store window.
The store looked closed for years.

I lost my way there once
In a Sunday kind of quiet,
Sunday kind of afternoon light
On a street of red-brick tenements.

How do you like that?
I said to no one.
How do you like that?
I said it again today upon waking.

That street went on forever
And all along I could feel the pins
In my back, prickling
The dark and heavy cloth.

St. Thomas Aquinas

I left parts of myself everywhere
The way absent-minded people leave
Gloves and umbrellas
Whose colors are sad from dispensing so much bad luck.

I was on a park bench asleep.
It was like the Art of Ancient Egypt.
I didn't wish to bestir myself.
I made my long shadow take the evening train.

"We give death to a child when we give it a doll,"
Said the woman who had read Djuna Barnes.
We whispered all night. She had traveled to darkest Africa.
She had many stories to tell about the jungle.

I was already in New York looking for work.
It was raining as in the days of Noah.
I stood in many doorways of that great city.
Once I asked a man in a tuxedo for a cigarette.
He gave me a frightened look and stepped out into the rain.

Since "man naturally desires happiness,"
According to St. Thomas Aquinas,
Who gave irrefutable proof of God's existence and purpose,
I loaded trucks in the Garment Center.
Me and a black man stole a woman's red dress.
It was of silk; it shimmered.

Upon a gloomy night with all our loving ardors on fire,
We carried it down the long empty avenue,
Each holding one sleeve.
The heat was intolerable, causing many terrifying human faces
To come out of hiding.

In the Public Library Reading Room
There was a single ceiling fan barely turning.
I had the travels of Herman Melville to serve me as a pillow.
I was on a ghost ship with its sails fully raised.
I could see no land anywhere.
The sea and its monsters could not cool me.

I followed a saintly-looking nurse into a doctor's office.
We edged past people with eyes and ears bandaged.
"I am a medieval philosopher in exile,"
I explained to my landlady that night.
And, truly, I no longer looked like myself.
I wore glasses with a nasty spider crack over one eye.

I stayed in the movies all day long.
A woman on the screen walked through a bombed city
Again and again. She wore army boots.
Her legs were long and bare. It was cold wherever she was.
She had her back turned to me, but I was in love with her.
I expected to find wartime Europe at the exit.

It wasn't even snowing! Everyone I met
Wore a part of my destiny like a carnival mask.
"I'm Bartleby the Scrivener," I told the Italian waiter.
"Me too," he replied.
And I could see nothing but overflowing ashtrays
The human-faced flies were busy examining.

A Letter

Dear philosophers, I get sad when I think.
Is it the same with you?
Just as I'm about to sink my teeth into the noumenon,
Some old girlfriend comes to distract me.
"She's not even alive!" I yell to heaven.

The wintry light made me go out of my way.
I saw beds covered with identical gray blankets.
I saw grim-looking men holding a naked woman
While they hosed her with cold water.
Was that to calm her nerves, or was it punishment?

I went to visit my friend Bob who said to me:
"We reach the real by overcoming the seduction of images."
I was overjoyed, until I realized
Such abstinence will never be possible for me.
I caught myself looking out the window.

Bob's father was taking their dog for a walk.
He moved with pain; the dog waited for him.
There was no one else in the park,
Only bare trees with an infinity of tragic shapes
To make thinking difficult.

Factory

The machines were gone, and so were those who
    worked them.
A single high-backed chair stood like a throne
In all that empty space.
I was on the floor making myself comfortable
For a long night of little sleep and much thinking.

An empty birdcage hung from a steam pipe.
In it I kept an apple and a small paring knife.
I placed newspapers all around me on the floor
So I could jump at the slightest rustle.
It was like the scratching of a pen,
The silence of the night writing in its diary.

Of rats who came to pay me a visit
I had the highest opinion.
They'd stand on two feet
As if about to make a polite request
On a matter of great importance.

Many other strange things came to pass.
Once a naked woman climbed on the chair
To reach the apple in the cage.
I was on the floor watching her go on tiptoe,
Her hand fluttering in the cage like a bird.

On other days, the sun peeked through dusty windowpanes
To see what time it was. But there was no clock,
Only the knife in the cage, glinting like a mirror,
And the chair in the far corner
Where someone once sat facing the brick wall.

Shelley

for M. Follain

Poet of the dead leaves driven like ghosts,
Driven like pestilence-stricken multitudes,
I read you first
One rainy evening in New York City,

In my atrocious Slavic accent,
Saying the mellifluous verses
From a battered, much-stained volume
I had bought earlier that day
In a secondhand bookstore on Fourth Avenue
Run by an initiate of the occult masters.

The little money I had being almost spent,
I walked the streets my nose in the book.
I sat in a dingy coffee shop
With last summer's dead flies on the table.
The owner was an ex-sailor
Who had grown a huge hump on his back

While watching the rain, the empty street.
He was glad to have me sit and read.
He'd refill my cup with a liquid dark as river Styx.

Shelley spoke of a mad, blind, dying king;
Of rulers who neither see, nor feel, nor know;
Of graves from which a glorious Phantom may
Burst to illumine our tempestuous day.

I too felt like a glorious phantom
Going to have my dinner
In a Chinese restaurant I knew so well.
It had a three-fingered waiter
Who'd bring my soup and rice each night
Without ever saying a word.

I never saw anyone else there.
The kitchen was separated by a curtain
Of glass beads which clicked faintly
Whenever the front door opened.
The front door opened that evening
To admit a pale little girl with glasses.

The poet spoke of the everlasting universe
Of things . . . of gleams of a remoter world
Which visit the soul in sleep . . .
Of a desert peopled by storms alone . . .

The streets were strewn with broken umbrellas
Which looked like funereal kites
This little Chinese girl might have made.
The bars on MacDougal Street were emptying.

There had been a fistfight.
A man leaned against a lamppost arms extended as if crucified,
The rain washing the blood off his face.

In a dimly lit side street,
Where the sidewalk shone like a ballroom mirror
At closing time —
A well-dressed man without any shoes
Asked me for money.
His eyes shone, he looked triumphant
Like a fencing master
Who had just struck a mortal blow.

How strange it all was . . . The world's raffle
That dark October night . . .
The yellowed volume of poetry
With its Splendors and Glooms
Which I studied by the light of storefronts:
Drugstores and barbershops,
Afraid of my small windowless room
Cold as a tomb of an infant emperor.

The Devils

You were a "victim of semiromantic anarchism
In its most irrational form."
I was "ill at ease in an ambiguous world

Deserted by Providence." We drank gin
And made love in the afternoon. The neighbors'
TVs were tuned to soap operas.

The unhappy couples spoke little.
There were interminable pauses.
Soft organ music. Someone coughing.

"It's like Strindberg's *Dream Play*," you said.
"What is?" I asked and got no reply.
I was watching a spider on the ceiling.

It was the kind St. Veronica ate in her martyrdom.
"That woman subsisted on spiders only,"
I told the janitor when he came to fix the faucet.

He wore dirty overalls and a derby hat.
Once he had been an inmate of a notorious state institution.
"I'm no longer Jesus," he informed us happily.

He believed only in devils now.
"This building is full of them," he confided.
One could see their horns and tails

If one caught them in their baths.
"He's got Dark Ages on his brain," you said.
"Who does?" I asked and got no reply.

The spider had the beginnings of a web
Over our heads. The world was quiet
Except when one of us took a sip of gin.

Crepuscule with Nellie

for Ira

Monk at the Five Spot
    late one night.
"Ruby, My Dear," "Epistrophy."
    The place nearly empty
Because of the cold spell.
One beautiful black transvestite
    alone up front,
Sipping his drink demurely.

The music Pythagorean,
    one note at a time
Connecting the heavenly spheres,
While I leaned against the bar
    surveying the premises
Through cigarette smoke.

All of a sudden, a clear sense
    of a memorable occasion . . .
The joy of it, the delicious melancholy . . .
This very strange man bent over the piano
    shaking his head, humming . . .

"Misterioso."

Then it was all over, thank you!
Chairs being stacked up on tables,
    their legs up.
The prospect of the freeze outside,
    the long walk home,
Making one procrastinatory.

Who said Americans don't have history,
    only endless nostalgia?
And where the hell was Nellie?

Two Dogs

for Charles and Holly

An old dog afraid of his own shadow
In some Southern town.
The story told me by a woman going blind,
One fine summer evening
As shadows were creeping
Out of the New Hampshire woods,
A long street with just a worried dog
And a couple of dusty chickens,
And all that sun beating down
In that nameless Southern town.

It made me remember the Germans marching
Past our house in 1944.
The way everybody stood on the sidewalk
Watching them out of the corner of the eye,
The earth trembling, death going by . . .
A little white dog ran into the street
And got entangled with the soldiers' feet.
A kick made him fly as if he had wings.
That's what I keep seeing!
Night coming down. A dog with wings.

Evening Talk

Everything you didn't understand
Made you what you are. Strangers
Whose eye you caught on the street
Studying you. Perhaps they were the all-seeing
Illuminati? They knew what you didn't,
And left you troubled like a strange dream.

Not even the light stayed the same.
Where did all that hard glare come from?
And the scent, as if mythical beings
Were being groomed and fed stalks of hay
On these roofs drifting among the evening clouds.

You didn't understand a thing!
You loved the crowds at the end of the day
That brought you so many mysteries.
There was always someone you were meant to meet
Who for some reason wasn't waiting.
Or perhaps they were? But not here, friend.

You should have crossed the street
And followed that obviously demented woman
With the long streak of blood-red hair
Which the sky took up like a distant cry.

The Betrothal

I found a key
In the street, someone's
House key
Lying there, glinting,

Long ago; the one
Who lost it
Is not going to remember it
Tonight, as I do.

It was a huge city
Of many dark windows,
Columns and domes.
I stood there thinking.

The street ahead of me
Shadowy, full of peril
Now that I held
The key. One or two

Late strollers
Unhurried and grave
In view. The sky above them
Of an unearthly clarity.

Eternity jealous
Of the present moment,
It occurred to me!
And then the moment was over.

Frightening Toys

History practicing its scissor-clips
In the dark,
So everything comes out in the end
Missing an arm or a leg.

Still, if that's all you've got
To play with today . . .
This doll at least had a head,
And its lips were red!

Frame houses like grim exhibits
Lining the empty street
Where a little girl sat on the steps
In a flowered nightgown, talking to it.

It looked like a serious matter,
Even the rain wanted to hear about it,
So it fell on her eyelashes,
And made them glisten.

The Big War

We played war during the war,
Margaret. Toy soldiers were in big demand,
The kind made from clay.
The lead ones they melted into bullets, I suppose.

You never saw anything as beautiful
As those clay regiments! I used to lie on the floor
For hours staring them in the eye.
I remember them staring back at me in wonder.

How strange they must have felt
Standing stiffly at attention
Before a large, uncomprehending creature
With a mustache made of milk.

In time they broke, or I broke them on purpose.
There was wire inside their limbs,
Inside their chests, but nothing in the heads!
Margaret, I made sure.

Nothing at all in the heads . . .
Just an arm, now and then, an officer's arm,
Wielding a saber from a crack
In my deaf grandmother's kitchen floor.

Death, the Philosopher

He gives excellent advice by example.
"See!" he says. "See that?"
And he doesn't have to open his mouth
To tell you what.
You can trust his vast experience.
Still, there's no huff in him.
Once he had a most unfortunate passion.
It came to an end.
He loved the way the summer dusk fell.
He wanted to have it falling forever.
It was not possible.

That was the big secret.
It's dreadful when things get as bad as that —
But then they don't!
He got the point, and so, one day,
Miraculously lucid, you, too, came to ask
About the strangeness of it all.
Charles, you said,
How strange you should be here at all!

First Thing in the Morning

To find a bit of thread
But twisted
In a peculiar way
And fallen
In an unlikely place

A black thread
Before the mystery
Of a closed door
The greater mystery
Of the four bare walls

And catch oneself thinking
Do I know anyone
Who wears such dark garments
Worn to threads
First thing in the morning?

The White Room

The obvious is difficult
To prove. Many prefer
The hidden. I did, too.
I listened to the trees.

They had a secret
Which they were about to
Make known to me,
And then didn't.

Summer came. Each tree
On my street had its own
Scheherazade. My nights
Were a part of their wild

Storytelling. We were
Entering dark houses,
More and more dark houses
Hushed and abandoned.

There was someone with eyes closed
On the upper floors.
The thought of it, and the wonder,
Kept me sleepless.

The truth is bald and cold,
Said the woman
Who always wore white.
She didn't leave her room much.

The sun pointed to one or two
Things that had survived
The long night intact.
The simplest things,

Difficult in their obviousness.
They made no noise.
It was the kind of day
People described as "perfect."

Gods disguising themselves
As black hairpins, a hand mirror,
A comb with a tooth missing?
No! That wasn't it.

Just things as they are,
Unblinking, lying mute
In that bright light—
And the trees waiting for the night.

Winter Sunset

Such skies came to worry men
On the eve of great battles
With clouds soaked in blood
Fleeing the armies of the night,

An old woman was summoned
Who could predict the future,
But she kept her mouth shut
Even when shown the naked sword.

In what remained of the light,
The white village church
Clutched its bird-shaped weathervane
Above the low rooftops.

A small child, who had been
Nursing at his mother's breast,
Hid his face from her
To see the horses rear in the sky.

The Pieces of the Clock Lie Scattered

So, hurry up!
The evening's coming.
The grownups are on the way.
There'll be hell to pay.

You forgot about time
While you sought its secret
In the slippery wheels,
Some of which had teeth.

You meant to enthrall
The girl across the hall.
She drew so near,
Her breast brushed your ear.

She ought to have gone home,
But you kept telling her
You'll have it together again
And ticking in no time.

Instead, you're under the table
Together, searching the floor.
Your hands are trembling,
And there's a key in the door.

The Immortal

You're shivering, O my memory.
You went out early and without a coat
To visit your old schoolmasters,
The cruel schoolmasters and their pet monkeys.
You took a wrong turn somewhere.
You met an army of gray days,
A ghost army of years on the march.
It was the bread they fed you,
The kind it takes a lifetime to chew.

You found yourself again on that street
Inside that small, rented room
With its single dusty window.
Outside it was snowing quietly,
Snowing and snowing for days on end.
You were ill and in bed.
Everyone else had gone to work.
The blind old woman next door,
Whose sighs and heavy steps you'd welcome now,
Had died mysteriously in the summer.

You had your own heartbeat to attend to.
You were perfectly alone and anonymous.
It would have taken months for anyone
To begin to miss you. The chill
Made you pull the covers up to your chin.

You remembered the lost arctic voyagers,
The evening snow erasing their footprints.
You had no money and no job.
Both of your lungs were hurting; still,
You had no intention of lifting a finger
To help yourself. You were immortal!

Outside, the same dark snowflake
Seemed to be falling over and over again.
You studied the cracked walls,
The maplike water stain on the ceiling,
Trying to fix in your mind its cities and rivers.

Time had stopped at dusk.
You were shivering at the thought
Of such great happiness.

At the Corner

The fat sisters
Kept a candy store
Dim and narrow
With dusty jars
Of jawbreaking candy.

We stayed thin, stayed
Glum, chewing gum
While staring at the floor,
The shoes of many strangers
Rushing in and out,

Making the papers outside
Flutter audibly
Under the lead weights,
Their headlines
Screaming in and out of view.

Cabbage

She was about to chop the head
In half,
But I made her reconsider
By telling her:
"Cabbage symbolizes mysterious love."

Or so said one Charles Fourier,
Who said many other strange and wonderful things,
So that people called him mad behind his back,

Whereupon I kissed the back of her neck
Ever so gently,

Whereupon she cut the cabbage in two
With a single stroke of her knife.

The Initiate

St. John of the Cross wore dark glasses
When he passed me on the street.
St. Therese of Ávila, beautiful and grave,
Came at me spreading her wings like a seagull.

"Lost soul," they both cried out,
"Where is your home?"

I was one of death's juggling balls.
The city was a mystic circus
With all of its lights dimmed,
The night's performance already started.

On a wide, poorly lit avenue,
Store windows waited for me,
Watched for me coming,
Knew what thoughts were on my mind.

In a church, where the child killer,
So the papers said,
Hid himself one night from the cold,
I sat in a pew blowing on my hands.

Like a thought forgotten till called forth —
The new snow on the sidewalk
Bore fresh footprints — some unknown master
Offering to guide my steps from now on.

In truth, I had no idea what was happening to me.
Four young hoods blocked my way,
Three dead serious,
One smiling crazily as he laid his hand on me.

I let them have my raincoat,
And went off telling myself
It was important to remain calm,
And to continue to observe oneself
As if one was a complete stranger.

At the address I'd been given,
There were white *X*'s painted on each window.
I knocked, but no one came to open.
By and by a girl joined me on the steps.
Her name was Alma, a propitious sign.

She knew a housewife
Who solved life's riddles
In a voice of a Sumerian queen.
We had a long chat about that
While shivering and stamping our feet.

In the sixteenth century, she told me,
Dabblers in occult sciences
Were roasted in iron cages,
Or else they were clothed in rags
And hanged on gibbets painted gold.

Once in a hotel room in Chicago, I confessed,
I caught sight of someone in the mirror
Who had my face,
But whose eyes I did not recognize —
Two hard, all-knowing eyes.

The hunger, the cold and the lack of sleep
Brought on a kind of ecstasy.
I walked the streets as if pursued by demons,
Trying to warm myself.

There was the East River,
There was the Hudson.
Their waters shone at midnight
Like oil in sanctuary lamps.

Something was about to happen to me
For which there would never be any words afterward.
I stood as if transfixed,
Watching the sky clear.

It was so quiet where I was,
You could hear a pin drop.
I thought I heard a pin drop
And went looking for it
In the dark, deserted city.

1986–2011

Paradise

In a neighborhood once called Hell's Kitchen
Where a beggar claimed to be playing Nero's fiddle
While the city burned in midsummer heat;
Where a lady barber who called herself Cleopatra
Wielded the scissors of fate over my head
Threatening to cut off my ears and nose;
Where a man and a woman went walking naked
In one of the dark side streets at dawn.

I must be dreaming, I told myself.
It was like meeting a couple of sphinxes.
I expected them to have wings, bodies of lions:
Him with his wildly tattooed chest;
Her with her huge, dangling breasts.

It happened so quickly, and so long ago!

You know that time just before the day breaks
When one yearns to lie down on cool sheets

In a room with shades drawn?
The hour when the beautiful suicides
Lying side by side in the morgue
Get up and walk out into the first light.

The curtains of cheap hotels flying out of windows
Like seagulls, but everything else quiet . . .
Steam rising out of the subway gratings . . .
Bodies glistening with sweat . . .
Madness, and you might even say, paradise!

In the Library

for Octavio

There's a book called
A Dictionary of Angels.
No one has opened it in fifty years,
I know, because when I did,
The covers creaked, the pages
Crumbled. There I discovered

The angels were once as plentiful
As species of flies.
The sky at dusk
Used to be thick with them.
You had to wave both arms
Just to keep them away.

Now the sun is shining
Through the tall windows.
The library is a quiet place.
Angels and gods huddled
In dark unopened books.

The great secret lies
On some shelf Miss Jones
Passes every day on her rounds.

She's very tall, so she keeps
Her head tipped as if listening.
The books are whispering.
I hear nothing, but she does.

The Wail

As if there were nothing to live for . . .
As if there were . . . nothing.
In the fading light, our mother
Sat sewing with her head bowed.

Did her hand tremble? By the first faint
Hint of night coming, how all lay
Still, except for the memory of that voice:
Him whom the wild life hurried away . . .

Long stretches of silence in between.
Clock talking to a clock.
Dogs lying on their paws with ears cocked.
You and me afraid to breathe.

Finally, she went to peek. Someone covered
With a newspaper on the sidewalk.
Otherwise, no one about. The street empty.
The sky full of homeless clouds.

The Scarecrow

God's refuted but the devil's not.

This year's tomatoes are something to see.
Bite into them, Martha,
As you would into a ripe apple.
After each bite add a little salt.

If the juices run down your chin
Onto your bare breasts,
Bend over the kitchen sink.

From there you can see your husband
Come to a dead stop in the empty field
Before one of his bleakest thoughts
Spreading its arms like a scarecrow.

Windy Evening

This old world needs propping up
When it gets this cold and windy.
The cleverly painted sets,
Oh, they're shaking badly!
They're about to come down.

There'll be nothing but infinite space then.
The silence supreme. Almighty silence.
Egyptian sky. Stars like torches
Of grave robbers entering the crypts of the kings.
Even the wind pausing, waiting to see.

Better grab hold of that tree, Lucille.
Its shape crazed, terror-stricken.
I'll hold the barn.
The chickens in it uneasy.
Smart chickens, rickety world.

V

from Hotel Insomnia

Evening Chess

The Black Queen raised high
In my father's angry hand.

The City

At least one crucified at every corner.
The eyes of a mystic, madman, murderer.
They know it's truly for nothing.
The eyes do. All the martyr's sufferings
On parade. Exalted mother of us all
Tending her bundles on the sidewalk,
Speaking to each as if it were a holy child.

There were many who saw none of this.
A couple lingered on kissing lustily
Right where someone lay under a newspaper.
His bloody feet, swollen twice their size,
Jutted out into the cold of the day,
Grim proofs of a new doctrine.

I tell you, I was afraid. A man screamed
And continued walking as if nothing had happened.
Everyone whose eyes I sought avoided mine.
Was I beginning to resemble him a little?
I had no answer to any of these questions.
Neither did the crucified on the next corner.

Stub of a Red Pencil

You were sharpened to a fine point
With a rusty razor blade.
Then the unknown hand swept the shavings
Into its moist palm
And disappeared from view.

You lay on the desk next to
The official-looking document
With a long list of names.
It was up to us to imagine the rest:
The high ceiling with its cracks
And odd-shaped water stains;
The window with its view
Of roofs covered with snow.

An inconceivable, varied world
Surrounding your severe presence
On every side,
Stub of a red pencil.

The Prodigal

Dark morning rain
Meant to fall
On a prison and a schoolyard,
Falling meanwhile
On my mother and her old dog.

How slow she shuffles now
In my father's Sunday shoes.
The dog by her side
Trembling with each step
As he tries to keep up.

I am on another corner waiting
With my head shaved.
My mind hops like a sparrow
In the rain.
I'm always watching and worrying about her.

Everything is a magic ritual,
A secret cinema,
The way she appears in a window hours later
To set the empty bowl
And spoon on the table,
And then exits
So that the day may pass,
And the night may fall
Into the empty bowl,
Empty room, empty house,
While the rain keeps
Knocking at the front door.

Hotel Insomnia

I liked my little hole,
Its window facing a brick wall.
Next door there was a piano.
A few evenings a month
A crippled old man came to play
"My Blue Heaven."

Mostly, though, it was quiet.
Each room with its spider in heavy overcoat
Catching his fly with a web
Of cigarette smoke and revery.
So dark,
I could not see my face in the shaving mirror.

At 5 A.M. the sound of bare feet upstairs.
The "Gypsy" fortuneteller,
Whose storefront is on the corner,
Going to pee after a night of love.
Once, too, the sound of a child sobbing.
So near it was, I thought
For a moment, I was sobbing myself.

The Inanimate Object

In my long late-night talks with the jailers, I raised again
the question of the object: Does it remain indifferent whether
it is perceived or not? (I had in mind the one concealed and
found posthumously while the newly vacated cell was fumi-
gated and swept.)

"Like a carved-wood demon of some nightmarish species,"
said one. "In cipher writ," said another. We were drinking a
homemade brew that made our heads spin. "When a neck but-
ton falls on the floor and hardly makes a sound," said the third
with a smile, but I said nothing.

"If only one could leave behind a little something to make
others stop and think," I thought to myself.

In the meantime, there was my piece of broken bottle to
worry about. It was green and had a deadly cutting edge. I no

longer remembered its hiding place, unless I had only dreamed of it, or this was another cell, another prison in an infinite series of prisons and long night talks with my jailers.

Outside Biaggi's Funeral Home

Three old women sat knitting
On the sidewalk
Every time I walked by.
Good evening, ladies,
I would say to them.
Good morning, too.
What a lovely time of year
To be alive!

While they stared at me,
The way house cats stare at a TV
When their owner is at work,
Two of them resuming their knitting,
The third watching me
Go my way
With her mouth hanging open.

And that was all.
I left the neighborhood and they stayed
Knitting away.
They could be still there today
For it's that kind of day,
Sweet and mild,
It made me think of them again
After a long, long while.

The Tiger

in memory of George Oppen

In San Francisco, that winter,
There was a dark little store
Full of sleepy Buddhas.
The afternoon I walked in,
No one came out to greet me.
I stood among the sages
As if trying to read their thoughts.

One was huge and made of stone.
A few were the size of a child's head
And had stains the color of dried blood.
There were even some no bigger than mice,
And they appeared to be listening.

"The winds of March, black winds,
The gritty winds," the dead poet wrote.

At sundown his street was empty
Except for my long shadow
Open before me like scissors.
There was his house where I told the story
Of the Russian soldier,
The one who looked Chinese.

He lay wounded in my father's bed,
And I brought him water and matches.
For that he gave me a little tiger
Made of ivory. Its mouth was open in anger,
But it had no stripes left.

There was the night when I colored
Its eyes black, its tongue red.
My mother held the lamp for me,
While worrying about the kind of luck
This beast might bring us.

The tiger in my hand growled faintly
When we were alone in the dark,
But when I put my ear to the poet's door
That afternoon, I heard nothing.

"The winds of March, black winds,
The gritty winds," he once wrote.

Clouds Gathering

It seemed the kind of life we wanted.
Wild strawberries and cream in the morning.
Sunlight in every room.
The two of us walking by the sea naked.

Some evenings, however, we found ourselves
Unsure of what comes next.
Like tragic actors in a theater on fire,
With birds circling over our heads,
The dark pines strangely still,
Each rock we stepped on bloodied by the sunset.

We were back on our terrace sipping wine.
Why always this hint of an unhappy ending?
Clouds of almost human appearance

Gathering on the horizon, but the rest lovely
With the air so mild and the sea untroubled.

The night suddenly upon us, a starless night.
You lighting a candle, carrying it naked
Into our bedroom and blowing it out quickly.
The dark pines and grasses strangely still.

Folk Songs

Sausage makers of History,
The bloody kind,
You all hail from a village
Where the dog barking at the moon
Is the only poet.

O King Oedipus, O Hamlet,
Fallen like flies
In the pot of cabbage soup,
No use beating with your fists,
Or sticking your tongues out.

Christ-faced spider on the wall
Darkened by evening shadows,
I spent my childhood on a cross
In a yard full of weeds,
White butterflies, and white chickens.

War

The trembling finger of a woman
Goes down the list of casualties
On the evening of the first snow.

The house is cold and the list is long.

All our names are included.

A Book Full of Pictures

Father studied theology through the mail
And this was exam time.
Mother knitted. I sat quietly with a book
Full of pictures. Night fell.
My hands grew cold touching the faces
Of dead kings and queens.

There was a black raincoat
    in the upstairs bedroom
Swaying from the ceiling,
But what was it doing there?
Mother's long needles made quick crosses.
They were black
Like the inside of my head just then.

The pages I turned sounded like wings.
"The soul is a bird," he once said.
In my book full of pictures

A battle raged: lances and swords
Made a kind of wintry forest
With my heart spiked and bleeding in its branches.

Evening Walk

You give the appearance of listening
To my thoughts, O trees,
Bent over the road I am walking
On a late-summer evening
When every one of you is a steep staircase
The night is slowly descending.

The high leaves like my mother's lips
Forever trembling, unable to decide,
For there's a bit of wind,
And it's like hearing voices,
Or a mouth full of muffled laughter,
A huge dark mouth we can all fit in
Suddenly covered by a hand.

Everything quiet. Light
Of some other evening strolling ahead,
Long-ago evening of silk dresses,
Bare feet, hair unpinned and falling.
Happy heart, what heavy steps you take
As you follow after them in the shadows.

The sky at the road's end cloudless and blue.
The night birds like children
Who won't come to dinner.
Lost children in the darkening woods.

Hotel Starry Sky

Millions of empty rooms with TV sets turned on.
I wasn't there, but I saw everything.
Titanic sinking like a birthday cake on the screen.
Poseidon, the night clerk, blowing out the candles
     one by one.

At three in the morning the gum machine in the lobby
With its cracked and defaced mirror
Is a new Madonna with her infant child
Wanting to know how much to tip the bellboy.

To Think Clearly

What I need is a pig and an angel.
The pig to stick his nose in a slop bucket,
The angel to scratch his back
And say sweet things in his ear.

The pig knows what's in store for him.
Give him hope, angel child,
With that foreverness stuff.
Don't go admiring yourself
In the butcher's knife
As if it were a whore's mirror,
Or tease him with a bloodstained apron
By raising it above your knees.

The pig has stopped eating
And stands among us thinking.

Already the crest of the rooster blazes
In the morning darkness.
He's not crowing but his eyes are fierce
As he struts across the yard.

The Chair

This chair was once a student of Euclid.

The book of his laws lay on its seat.
The schoolhouse windows were open,
So the wind turned the pages
Whispering the glorious proofs.

The sun set over the golden roofs.
Everywhere the shadows lengthened,
But Euclid kept quiet about that.

Missing Child

You of the dusty, sun-yellowed picture
I saw twenty years ago
Inside the window of a dry-cleaning store,
I thought of you again tonight
Sitting by the window,
Watching the street,
As your mother must've done every night,

And still does, for all I know.
The sky cloudy, and now even
The rain beginning to fall

On the same old city, the same old street
With its padlocked, dimly lit store,
And your thin, pale face
Next to the poster for a firemen's ball.

Marina's Epic

The Eskimos were ravaging Peru,
Grandfather fought the Huns,
Mother sold firecrackers to Bedouins.

We were inmates of an orphanage in Kraków;
A prison in Panama;
A school for beggars in Genoa.

In Japan I was taught how to catch ghosts
With chopsticks.
In Amsterdam we saw a Christmas tree
In a whorehouse window.

My sister roamed French battlefields in World War I
Rescuing ladybugs.
She'd carry the shivering insect
Into a village church and leave it in care of a saint.

In Paris, we knew a Russian countess
Who scrubbed floors at the opera
With a red rose between her teeth.

Father played a dead man in a German movie.
It was silent. The piano player looked like
Edgar Allan Poe wearing a Moroccan fez.

On the back of a large suitcase
We sailed the stormy Atlantic one February
Taking turns to mend the rips in our grandmother's
    wedding dress,
We used as a sail.

The next thing we knew,
We were outside a pink motel in Arizona singing:
"We love you, life,
Even though you're always laughing at us."

One day, we joined some Tibetan monks.
They had a holy mountain
From which one could see all of Los Angeles.

A meal of Sardinian goat cheese, Greek olives,
Spanish wine and black Russian bread,
Because talking about the past makes one hungry.

In New York, the movie screens were as big as the pyramids.
Broadway was a river as wide as the Nile
Crowded with barges and pleasure boats
Carrying Cleopatras and her beaus for a night on the town.

We stood on the corner of Forty-second Street
Peddling vials of gypsy love potion and statues of African gods,
And waiting for General Washington
To ride by on his white horse and nod in our direction.

Lost Glove

Here's a woman's black glove.
It ought to mean something.
A thoughtful stranger left it
On the red mailbox at the corner.

Three days the sky was troubled,
Then today a few snowflakes fell
On the glove, which someone,
In the meantime, had turned over,
So that its fingers could close

A little . . . Not yet a fist.
So I waited, with the night coming.
Something told me not to move.
Here where flames rise from trash barrels,
And the homeless sleep standing up.

Romantic Sonnet

Evenings of sovereign clarity—
Wine and bread on the table,
Mother praying,
Father naked in bed.

Was I that skinny boy stretched out
In the field behind the house,
His heart cut out with a toy knife?
Was I the crow hovering over him?

Happiness, you are the bright red lining
Of the dark winter coat
Grief wears inside out.

This is about myself when I'm remembering,
And your long insomniac's nails,
O Time, I keep chewing and chewing.

Beauty

I'm telling you, this was the real thing, the same one they
kicked out of Aesthetics, told her she didn't exist!

O you simple, indefinable, ineffable, and so forth. I like
your black apron, and your new Chinese girl's hairdo. I also
like naps in the afternoon, well-chilled white wine, and the
squabbling of philosophers.

What joy and happiness you give us each time you reach
over the counter to take our money, so we catch a whiff of your
breath. You've been chewing on sesame crackers and garlic
salami, divine creature!

When I heard the old man, Plotinus, say something about
"every soul wanting to possess you," I gave him a dirty look,
and rushed home to unwrap and kiss the pink ham you sliced
for me with your own hand.

My Quarrel with the Infinite

I preferred the fleeting,
Like a memory of a sip of wine
Of noble vintage
On the tongue with eyes closed . . .

When you tapped me on the shoulder,
O light, unsayable in your splendor.
A lot of good you did to me.
You just made my insomnia last longer.

I sat rapt at the spectacle,
Secretly ruing the fugitive:
All its provisory, short-lived
Kisses and enchantments.

Here with the new day breaking,
And a single scarecrow on the horizon
Directing the traffic
Of crows and their shadows.

The Old World

for Dan and Jeanne

I believe in the soul; so far
It hasn't made much difference.
I remember an afternoon in Sicily.
The ruins of some temple.
Columns fallen in the grass like naked lovers.

The olives and goat cheese tasted delicious
And so did the wine
With which I toasted the coming night,
The darting swallows,
The Saracen wind and moon.

It got darker. There was something
Long before there were words:

The evening meal of shepherds . . .
A fleeting whiteness among the trees . . .
Eternity eavesdropping on time.

The goddess going to bathe in the sea.
She must not be followed.
These rocks, these cypress trees,
May be her old lovers.
Oh to be one of them, the wine whispered to me.

Country Fair

for Hayden Carruth

If you didn't see the six-legged dog,
It doesn't matter.
We did and he mostly lay in the corner.
As for the extra legs,

One got used to them quickly
And thought of other things.
Like, what a cold, dark night
To be out at the fair.

Then the keeper threw a stick
And the dog went after it
On four legs, the other two flapping behind,
Which made one girl shriek with laughter.

She was drunk and so was the man
Who kept kissing her neck.
The dog got the stick and looked back at us.
And that was the whole show.

VI

from A Wedding in Hell

Miracle Glass Co.

Heavy mirror carried
Across the street,
I bow to you
And to everything that appears in you,
Momentarily
And never again the same way:

This street with its pink sky,
Row of gray tenements,
A lone dog,
Children on rollerskates,
Woman buying flowers,
Someone looking lost.

In you, mirror framed in gold
And carried across the street
By someone I can't even see,
To whom, too, I bow.

Late Arrival

The world was already here
Serene in its otherness.
It only took you to arrive
On the afternoon train
To where no one awaited you.

A town no one ever remembered.
Because of its ordinariness

Where you lost your way
Searching for a place to stay
In a maze of identical streets.

It was then that you heard,
As if for the very first time,
The sound of your own footsteps
Passing a church clock
Which had stopped at one

On the corner of two streets
Emptied by the hot sun.
Two glimpses of the eternal
For you to wonder about
Before resuming your walk.

Tattooed City

I, who am only an incomprehensible
Bit of scribble
On some warehouse wall
Or some subway entrance.

Matchstick figure,
Heart pierced by arrow,
Scratch of a meter maid
On a parked hearse.

CRAZY CHARLIE in red spraypaint
Crowding for warmth
With other unknown divinities
In an underpass at night.

Dream Avenue

Monumental, millennial decrepitude,
As tragedy requires. A broad
Avenue with trash unswept,
A few solitary speck-sized figures
Going about their business
In a world already smudged by a schoolboy's eraser.

You've no idea what city this is,
What country? It could be a dream,
But is it yours? You're nothing
But a vague sense of loss,
A piercing, heart-wrenching dread
On an avenue with no name

With a few figures conveniently small
And blurred who, in any case,
Appear to have their backs to you
As they look elsewhere, beyond
The long row of gray buildings and their many windows,
Some of which appear broken.

Haunted Mind

Savageries to come,
Cities smelling of death already,
What idol will you worship,
Whose icy heart?

One cold Thursday night,
In a neighborhood dive,
I watched the Beast of War
Lick its sex on TV.

There were three other customers:
Mary sitting in old Joe's lap,
Her crazy son in the corner
With arms spread wide over the pinball machine.

Paradise Motel

Millions were dead; everybody was innocent.
I stayed in my room. The president
Spoke of war as of a magic love potion.
My eyes were opened in astonishment.
In a mirror my face appeared to me
Like a twice-canceled postage stamp.

I lived well, but life was awful.
There were so many soldiers that day,
So many refugees crowding the roads.
Naturally, they all vanished
With a touch of the hand.
History licked the corners of its bloody mouth.

On the pay channel, a man and a woman
Were trading hungry kisses and tearing off
Each other's clothes while I looked on
With the sound off and the room dark
Except for the screen where the color
Had too much red in it, too much pink.

A Wedding in Hell

They were pale like the stones on the meadow
The black sheep lick.
Pale stones like children in their Sunday clothes
Playing at bride and groom.

There we found a clock face with Roman numerals
In the old man's overcoat pocket.
He kept looking at the sky without recognizing it,
And now it was time for a little rain to fall.

Your sheltering hands, Mother, which made the old man
    disappear.
The Lord who saw over them
Saw into our hearts while we unlaced his boots.

I'm turning off the lights so His eyes won't find you, you said.
O dreams like evening shadows on a windy meadow,
And your hands, Mother, like white mice.

The Dead in Photographs

All they could do is act innocent
Standing still for the camera,
Only a few of them thinking to move
And leave a blur for posterity.

Others held their smiles forever.
The groom with a suit too big for him,
And his bride with a small straw hat
And a topping of strawberries.

In Los Angeles, one Sunday morning,
The photographer took a picture
Of a closed barbershop
And a black cat crossing an empty avenue,

A blind man outside a bus station
Playing the guitar and singing,
A little boy walking up to the camera
Smiling and sticking his tongue out.

Madame Thebes

That awful deceit of appearances.
Some days
Everything looks unfamiliar
On my street.
It's somebody else's life I'm living.

An immaculate silent order
Of white buildings and dark clouds,
And then the open door
In a house with lowered voices.
Someone left in a hurry,
And they're waiting for me to come in
With a lit match.

There's a rustle of a long skirt,
But when I enter
It's only the evening papers
Sliding off the table
Birdlike
In a large and drafty
And now altogether empty room.

Evening Visitor

You remind me of those dwarfs in Velázquez.
Former dogcatcher
Promoted to professor at a correspondence school
With a matchbook address.

That couple screwing and watching
Themselves in the mirror,
Do you approve of them
As they gasp and roll their eyes in ecstasy?

And how about the solitary wine drinker?
He's drinking because he can't decide
Whether to kill only one of them or both—
And here it's already morning!

Some damn bird chirping in the trees.
Is that it? I beseech you. Answer me!

The Massacre of the Innocents

The poets of the Late Tang Dynasty
Could do nothing about it except to write:
"On the western hills the sun sets . . .
Horses blown by the whirlwind tread the clouds."

I could not help myself either. I felt joy
Even at the sight of a crow circling over me
As I stretched out on the grass
Alone now with the silence of the sky.

Only the wind making a slight rustle
As it turned the pages of the book by my side,
Back and forth, searching for something
For that bloody crow to read.

Pascal's Idea

My insignificance is a sign of my greatness.
Marvel, draw back
As I scurry in my roachlike way
Through these greasy kitchens
With their raised knives
And their fat-assed cooks
Bent over steaming pots.

My life is a triumph over the world's connivances
And blind chance.
I found the poison you left for me
Extremely nourishing.

Once I sipped milk out of a saucer left for the cat.
Once I ran across a birthday cake
With its candles already lit.
It was terrifying
And I suppose a bit like
What your heaven and hell combined must be.

The Clocks of the Dead

One night I went to keep the clock company.
It had a loud tick after midnight

As if it were uncommonly afraid.
It's like whistling past a graveyard,
I explained.
In any case, I told him I understood.

Once there were clocks like that
In every kitchen in America.
Now the factory's windows are all broken.
The old men on night shift are in Charon's boat.
The day you stop, I said to the clock,
The little wheels they keep in reserve
Will have rolled away
Into many hard-to-find places.

Just thinking about it, I forgot to wind the clock.
We woke up in the dark.
How quiet the city is, I said.
Like the clocks of the dead, my wife replied.
Grandmother on the wall,
I heard the snows of your childhood
Begin to fall.

Wanted Poster

From the closed, block-long post office
I heard him whisper
Out of his flyspecked mouth
As I hurried by on the street.
Hunted beast, he said,
His eyes dark and mean under the rusty thumbtacks.
Who furloughed you today
To go around grinning at every woman you meet?

Explaining a Few Things

Every worm is a martyr,
Every sparrow subject to injustice,
I said to my cat,
Since there was no one else around.

It's raining. In spite of their huge armies
What can the ants do?
And the roach on the wall
Like a waiter in an empty restaurant?

I'm going in the cellar
To stroke the rat caught in a trap.
You watch the sky.
If it clears, scratch on the door.

The Supreme Moment

As an ant is powerless
Against a raised boot,
And only has an instant
To have a bright idea or two.
The black boot so polished,
He can see himself
Reflected in it, distorted,
Perhaps made larger
Into a huge monster ant
Shaking his arms and legs
Threateningly?

The boot may be hesitating,
Demurring, having misgivings,
Gathering cobwebs,
Dew?
Yes, and apparently no.

Crazy About Her Shrimp

We don't even take time
To come up for air.
We keep our mouths full and busy
Eating bread and cheese
And smooching in between.

No sooner have we made love
Than we are back in the kitchen.
While I chop the hot peppers,
She wiggles her ass
And stirs the shrimp on the stove.

How good the wine tastes
That has run red
Out of a laughing mouth!
Down her chin
And onto her naked tits.

"I'm getting fat," she says,
Turning this way and that way
Before the mirror.
"I'm crazy about her shrimp!"
I shout to the gods above.

Transport

In the frying pan
On the stove
I found my love
And me naked.

Chopped onions
Fell on our heads
And made us cry.
It's like a parade,
I told her, confetti
When some guy
Reaches the moon.

"Means of transport,"
She replied obscurely
While we fried.
"Means of transport!"

Love Flea

He took a flea
From her armpit
To keep

And cherish
In a matchbox,
Even pricking his finger

From time to time
To feed it
Drops of blood.

What I Overheard

In summer's idle time,
When trees grow heavy with leaves
And spread shade everywhere
That is a delight to lie in
Alone
Or in the company of a dear friend,

Dreaming or having a quiet talk
Without looking at each other,
Until she feels drowsy
As if after too much wine,
And you draw close for a kiss
On her cheek, and instead
Stay with lips pursed, listening

To a bee make its rounds lazily,
And a far-off rooster crow
On the edge of sleep with the leaves hushed
Or rustling, ever so softly,
About something or other on their mind.

Leaves

Lovers who take pleasure
In the company of trees,
Who seek diversion after many kisses
In each other's arms,
Watching the leaves,

The way they quiver
At the slightest breath of wind,
The way they thrill,
And shudder almost individually,
One of them beginning to shake
While the others are still quiet,
Unaccountably, unreasonably—

What am I saying?
One leaf in a million more fearful,
More happy,
Than all the others?

On this oak tree casting
Such deep shade,
And my lids closing sleepily
With that one leaf twittering
Now darkly, now luminously.

Paper Dolls Cut Out of a Newspaper

Four of them holding hands like a family.
There's news of war this morning
And an ad for a coffee they call heavenly
Next to the picture of the president.

Hold them up for us to see, little Rosie.
Hold them up a bit longer.
Watch them dance, watch them trip
And make your grandparents laugh

With their knives and forks in the air,
While printer's ink comes off your fingers
And blackens your face
As you hurry to cover your eyes.

Reading History

for Hans Magnus

At times, reading here
In the library,
I'm given a glimpse
Of those condemned to death
Centuries ago,
And of their executioners.
I see each pale face before me
The way a judge
Pronouncing a sentence would,
Marveling at the thought
That I do not exist yet.

With eyes closed I can hear
The evening birds.
Soon they will be quiet
And the final night on earth
Will commence
In the fullness of its sorrow.

How vast, dark, and impenetrable
Are the early-morning skies
Of those led to their death
In a world from which I'm entirely absent,
Where I can still watch
Someone's slumped back,

Someone who is walking away from me
With his hands tied,
His graying head still on his shoulders,
Someone who
In what little remains of his life
Knows in some vague way about me,
And thinks of me as God,
As devil.

Psalm

You've been making up your mind a long time,
O Lord, about these madmen
Running the world. Their reach is long,
And their sharp claws may have frightened you.

One of them just cast a shadow over me.
The day turned chill. I dangled
Between terror and speechless fury
In the corner of my son's bedroom.

I sought with my eyes you, in whom I do not believe.
You've been busy making the flowers pretty,
The lambs run after their mother,
Or perhaps you haven't been doing even that?

It was spring. The killers were full of determination
And high spirits, and your clergymen
Were right at their side, making sure
Our last words didn't include a curse on you.

Empires

My grandmother prophesied the end
Of your empires, O fools!
She was ironing. The radio was on.
The earth trembled beneath our feet.

One of your heroes was giving a speech.
"Monster," she called him.
There were cheers and gun salutes for the monster.
"I could kill him with my bare hands,"
She announced to me.

There was no need to. They were all
Going to the devil any day now.
"Don't go blabbering about this to anyone,"
She warned me.
And pulled my ear to make sure I understood.

Romantic Landscape

To grieve, always to suffer
At the thought of time passing.
The outside world shadowy
As your deepest self.
Melancholy meadows, trees so still,
They seem afraid of themselves.

The sunset sky for one brief moment
Radiant with some supreme insight,
And then it's over. Tragic theater:
Blood and mourning at which
Even the birds fall silent.

Spirit, you who are everywhere and nowhere,
Watch over the lost lamb
Now that the mouth of the Infinite
Opens over us
And its dumb tongue begins to move darkly.

Mystics

Help me to find what I've lost,
If it was ever, however briefly, mine,
You who may have found it.
Old man praying in the privy,
Lonely child drawing a secret room
And in it a stopped clock.

Seek to convey its truth to me
By hints and omens.
The room in shadow, perhaps the wrong room?
The cockroach on the wall,
The naked lovers kissing
On the TV with the sound off.
I could hear the red faucet drip.

Or else restore to plain view
What is eternally invisible
And speaks by being silent.
Blue distances to the north,
The fires of the evening to the west,
Christ himself in pain, panhandling
On the altar of the storefront church
With a long bloody nail in each palm.

In this moment of amazement . . .
Since I do ask for it humbly,
Without greed, out of true need.
My teeth chattered so loudly,
My old dog got up to see what's the matter.
Oh divine lassitude, long drawn-out sigh
As the vision came and went.

Imported Novelties

They didn't answer to repeated knocks,
Or perhaps they were in no hurry.
On the eighteenth floor
Even the sunlight moved lazily

Past the floating dust.
A year could pass here, I thought,
As in a desert solitude.

"Unknown parties, rarely seen,"
The elevator operator warned me.
He wore a New Year's party hat in August;
I was looking for work.

Inside, I imagined rows of file cabinets,
Old desks, dead telephones.
I could have been sitting at one of them myself,
Like someone doused with gasoline
In the moment before the match is lit,

But then the elevator took me down.

Via del Tritone

In Rome, on the street of that name,
I was walking alone in the sun
In the noonday heat, when I saw a house
With shutters closed, the sight of which
Pained me so much, I could have
Been born there and left inconsolably.

The ochre walls, the battered old door
I was tempted to push open and didn't,
Knowing already the coolness of the entrance,
The garden with a palm tree beyond,
And the dark stairs on the left.

Shutters closed to cool shadowy rooms
With impossibly high ceilings,
And here and there a watery mirror
And my pale and contorted face
To greet me and startle me again and again.

"You found what you were looking for,"
I expected someone to whisper.
But there was no one, neither there
Nor in the street, which was deserted
In that monstrous heat that gives birth
To false memories and tritons.

Shaving

Child of sorrow.
Old snotnose.
Stray scrap from the table of the gods.
Toothless monkey.
Workhorse,
Wheezing there,
Coughing too.

The trouble with you is,
Your body and soul
Don't get along well together.
Pigsty for a brain,
Stop them from making faces at each other
In the mirror!
Then, take off these silly angel wings
From your gorilla suit.

Trailer Park

Lewis and Clark,
You never found anything
To compare.
Trees without leaves,
Naked branches,
And then a snowflake or two
In flight
From the darkening sky.

End of town,
No sign of life
In any of the trailers
As you drive by slowly,
The ground bare,
Frozen
This overcast morning
While he squats absorbed
In a game.

A small child bent over a toy
On a road to Calvary.
In the distance, the crows
Already perched
On crosses
Of unknown prophets
And thieves.

The Tower

Five, six chairs piled up in the yard
And you on top of them
Sitting like a hanging judge,
Wearing only pajama bottoms.

The sparrows, what must they think?
If people are watching,
They are as quiet as goldfish,
Or expensive cuts of meat.

Hour after hour alone with the sky
And its mad serenity
On the rickety, already teetering,
Already leaning tower.

How frightened the neighbors must be.
Not even a child walks the streets
In this heat,
Not even a car passes and slows down.

What do you see in the distance, O father?
A windowpane struck by the setting sun?
A game called on account of darkness?
The players like fleas in a convent.

Hell's bells about to toll?

The Secret

I have my excuse, Mr. Death,
The old note my mother wrote
The day I missed school.
Snow fell. I told her my head hurt
And my chest. The clock struck
The hour. I lay in my father's bed
Pretending to be asleep.

Through the window I could see
The snow-covered roofs. In my mind
I rode a horse; I was in a ship
On a stormy sea. Then I dozed off.
When I woke, the house was still.
Where was my mother?
Had she written the note and left?

I rose and went searching for her.
In the kitchen our white cat sat
Picking at the bloody head of a fish.
In the bathroom the tub was full,
The mirror and the window fogged over.

When I wiped them, I saw my mother
In her red bathrobe and slippers
Talking to a soldier on the street
While the snow went on falling,
And she put a finger
To her lips, and held it there.

VII

from Walking the Black Cat

Mirrors at 4 A.M.

You must come to them sideways
In rooms webbed in shadow,
Sneak a view of their emptiness
Without them catching
A glimpse of you in return.

The secret is,
Even the empty bed is a burden to them,
A pretense.
They are more themselves keeping
The company of a blank wall,
The company of time and eternity

Which, begging your pardon,
Cast no image
As they admire themselves in the mirror,
While you stand to the side
Pulling a hanky out
To wipe your brow surreptitiously.

Relaxing in a Madhouse

They had already attached the evening's tears to the
windowpanes.
The general was busy with the ant farm in his head.
The holy saints in their tombs were resting, all except
one who was a prisoner of a dark-haired movie star.
Moses wore a false beard and so did Lincoln.

X reproduced the Socratic method of interrogation by demonstrating the ceiling's ignorance.

"They stole the secret of the musical matchbook from me," confided Adam.

"The world's biggest rooster was going to make me famous," said Eve.

Oh to run naked over the darkening meadow after the cold shower!

In the white pavilion the nurse was turning water into wine.

Hurry home, dark cloud.

Emily's Theme

My dear trees, I no longer recognize you
In that wintry light.
You brought me a reminder I can do without:
The world is old, it was always old,
There's nothing new in it this afternoon.
The garden could've been a padlocked window
Of a pawnshop I was studying
With every item in it dust-covered.

Each one of my thoughts was being ghostwritten
By anonymous authors. Each time they hit
A cobwebbed typewriter key, I shudder.
Luckily, dark came quickly today.
Soon the neighbors were burning leaves,
And perhaps a few other things too.
Later, I saw the children run around the fire,
Their faces demonic in its flames.

Cameo Appearance

I had a small, nonspeaking part
In a bloody epic. I was one of the
Bombed and fleeing humanity.
In the distance our great leader
Crowed like a rooster from a balcony,
Or was it a great actor
Impersonating our great leader?

That's me there, I said to the kiddies.
I'm squeezed between the man
With two bandaged hands raised
And the old woman with her mouth open
As if she were showing us a tooth

That hurts badly. The hundred times
I rewound the tape, not once
Could they catch sight of me
In that huge gray crowd,
That was like any other gray crowd.

Trot off to bed, I said finally.
I know I was there. One take
Is all they had time for.
We ran, and the planes grazed our hair,
And then they were no more
As we stood dazed in the burning city,
But, of course, they didn't film that.

The Friends of Heraclitus

Your friend has died, with whom
You roamed the streets,
At all hours, talking philosophy.
So, today you went alone,
Stopping often to change places
With your imaginary companion,
And argue back against yourself
On the subject of appearances:
The world we see in our heads
And the world we see daily,
So difficult to tell apart
When grief and sorrow bow us over.

You two often got so carried away
You found yourselves in strange neighborhoods
Lost among unfriendly folk,
Having to ask for directions
While on the verge of a supreme insight,
Repeating your question
To an old woman or a child
Both of whom may have been deaf and dumb.

What was that fragment of Heraclitus
You were trying to remember
As you stepped on the butcher's cat?
Meantime, you yourself were lost
Between someone's new black shoe
Left on the sidewalk
And the sudden terror and exhilaration
At the sight of a girl
Dressed up for a night of dancing
Speeding by on roller skates.

An Address with Exclamation Points

I accused History of gluttony;
Happiness of anorexia!

O History, cruel and mystical,
You ate Russia as if it were
A pot of white beans cooked with
Sausage, smoked ribs and ham hocks!

O Happiness, whose every miserly second
Is brimming with eternity!
You sat over a dish of vanilla custard
Without ever touching it!

The silent heavens were peeved!
They made the fair skies at sunset
Flash their teeth and burp from time to time,
Till our wedding picture slid off the wall.

The kitchen is closed! the waiters shouted.
No more vineyard snails in garlic butter!
No more ox tripe fried in onions!
We have only tears of happiness left!

What the Gypsies Told My Grandmother
While She Was Still a Young Girl

War, illness and famine will make you their favorite grandchild.
You'll be like a blind person watching a silent movie.
You'll chop onions and pieces of your heart into the same
     hot skillet.
Your children will sleep in a suitcase tied with a rope.

Your husband will kiss your breasts every night as if they were
    two gravestones.

Already the crows are grooming themselves for you and your
    people.
Your oldest son will lie with flies on his lips without smiling or
    lifting his hand.
You'll envy every ant you meet in your life and every roadside
    weed.
Your body and soul will sit on separate stoops chewing the
    same piece of gum.

Little cutie, are you for sale? the devil will say.
The undertaker will buy a toy for your grandson.
Your mind will be a hornet's nest even on your deathbed.
You will pray to God but God will hang a sign that He's not to
    be disturbed.
Question no further, that's all I know.

Little Unwritten Book

Rocky was a regular guy, a loyal friend.
The trouble was he was only a cat.
Let's practice, he'd say, and he'd pounce
On his shadow on the wall.
I have to admit, I didn't learn a thing.
I often sat watching him sleep.
If the birds tried to have a bit of fun in the yard,
He opened one eye.
I even commended him for good behavior.

He was black except for the white gloves he wore.
He played the piano in the parlor

By walking over its keys back and forth.
With exquisite tact he chewed my ear
If I wouldn't get up from my chair.
Then one day he vanished. I called.
I poked in the bushes.
I walked far into the woods.

The mornings were the hardest. I'd put out
A saucer of milk at the back door.
Peekaboo, a bird called out. She knew.
At one time we had ten farmhands working for us.
I'd make a megaphone with my hands and call.
I still do, though it's been years.
Rocky! I cry.
And now the bird is silent too.

Have You Met Miss Jones?

I have. At the funeral
Pulling down her skirt to cover her knees
While inadvertently
Showing us her cleavage
Down to the tip of her nipples.

A complete stranger, wobbly on her heels,
Negotiating the exit
With the assembled mourners
Eyeing her rear end
With visible interest.

Presidential hopefuls
Will continue to lie to the people
As we sit here bowed.

New hatreds will sweep the globe
Faster than the weather.
Sewer rats will sniff around
Lit cash machines
While we sigh over the departed.

And her beauty will live on, no matter
What any one of these black-clad,
Grim veterans of every wake,
Every prison gate and crucifixion,
Sputters about her discourtesy.

Miss Jones, you'll be safe
With the insomniacs. You'll triumph
Where they pour wine from a bottle
Wrapped in a white napkin,
Eat sausage with pan-fried potatoes,
And grow misty-eyed remembering

The way you walked past the open coffin,
Past the stiff with his nose in the air
Taking his long siesta.
A cute little number, an old man said,
But who was she?
Miss Jones, the guest book proclaimed.

Charm School

Madame Gabrielle, were you really French?
And what were those heavy books
You made them balance on top of their heads,

Young women with secret aspirations,
We saw strolling past the row of windows
In the large room above Guido's barbershop?

On the same floor was the office of an obscure
Weekly preaching bloody revolution.
Men with raised collars and roving eyes
Wandered in and out. When they conspired
They spat and pulled down the yellow shades,
Not to raise them or open the windows again

Until the summer heat came and your students
Wore dresses with their shoulders bared
As they promenaded with books on their heads,
And the bald customer in the barbershop
Sat sweating while overseeing in the mirror
His three remaining hairs being combed.

Ghosts

It's Mr. Brown looking much better
Than he did in the morgue.
He's brought me a huge carp
In a bloodstained newspaper.
What an odd visit.
I haven't thought of him in years.

Linda is with him and so is Sue.
Two pale and elegant fading memories
Holding each other by the hand.
Even their lipstick is fresh
Despite all the scientific proofs
To the contrary.

Is Linda going to cook the fish?
She turns and gazes in the direction
Of the kitchen while Sue
Continues to watch me mournfully.
I don't believe any of it,
And still I'm scared stiff.

I know of no way to respond,
So I do nothing.
The windows are open. The air's thick
With the scent of magnolias.
Drops of evening rain are dripping
From the dark and heavy leaves.
I take a deep breath; I close my eyes.

Dear specters, I don't even believe
You are here, so how is it
You're making me comprehend
Things I would rather not know just yet?

It's the way you stare past me
At what must already be my own ghost,
Before taking your leave,
As unexpectedly as you came in,
Without one of us breaking the silence.

Café Paradiso

My chicken soup thickened with pounded young almonds
My blend of winter greens.
Dearest tagliatelle with mushrooms, fennel, anchovies,
Tomatoes and vermouth sauce.

Beloved monkfish braised with onions, capers
And green olives.
Give me your tongue tasting of white beans and garlic,
Sexy little assortment of formaggi and frutta!
I want to drown with you in red wine like a pear,
Then sleep in a macédoine of wild berries with cream.

At the Cookout

The wives of my friends
Have the air
Of having shared a secret.
Their eyes are lowered
But when we ask them
What for
They only glance at each other
And smile,
Which only increases our desire
To know . . .

Something they did
Long ago,
Heedless of the consequences,
That left
Such a lingering sweetness?

Is that the explanation
For the way
They rest their chins
In the palms of their hands,
Their eyes closed
In the summer heat?

Come tell us,
Or give us a hint.
Trace a word or just a single letter
In the wine
Spilled on the table.

No reply. Both of them
Lovey-dovey
With the waning sunlight
And the evening breeze
On their faces.

The husbands drinking
And saying nothing,
Dazed and mystified as they are
By their wives' power
To give
And take away happiness,
As if their heads
Were crawling with snakes.

Pastoral Harpsichord

A house with a screened-in porch
On the road to nowhere.
The missus topless because of the heat,
A bag of Frito Banditos in her lap.
President Bush on TV
Watching her every bite.

Poor reception, that's the one
Advantage we have here,
I said to the mutt lying at my feet

And sighing in sympathy.
On another channel the preacher
Came chaperoned by his ghost
When he shut his eyes full of tears
To pray for dollars.

"Bring me another beer," I said to her ladyship,
And when she wouldn't oblige,
I went out to make chamber music
Against the sunflowers in the yard.

Entertaining the Canary

Yellow feathers,
Is it true
You chirp to the cop
On the beat?

Desist. Turn your
Nervous gaze
At the open bathroom door
Where I'm soaping

My love's back
And putting my chin on her shoulder
So I can do the same for her
Breasts and crotch.

Sing. Flutter your wings
As if you were applauding,
Or I'll drape her black slip
Over your gilded cage.

Slaughterhouse Flies

Evenings, they ran their bloody feet
Over the pages of my schoolbooks.
With eyes closed, I can still hear
The trees on our street
Saying a moody farewell to summer,

And someone, under our window, recalling
The silly old cows hesitating,
Growing suddenly suspicious
Just as the blade drops down on them.

Blood Orange

It looks so dark the end of the world may be near.
I believe it's going to rain.
The birds in the park are silent.
Nothing is what it seems to be,
Nor are we.

There's a tree on our street so big
We can all hide in its leaves.
We won't need any clothes either.
I feel as old as a cockroach, you said.
In my head, I'm a passenger on a ghost ship.

Not even a sigh outdoors now.
If a child was left on our doorstep,
It must be asleep.
Everything is teetering on the edge of everything
With a polite smile.

It's because there are things in this world
That just can't be helped, you said.
Right then, I heard the blood orange
Roll off the table and with a thud
Lie cracked open on the floor.

October Light

That same light by which I saw her last
Made me close my eyes now in revery,
Remembering how she sat in the garden

With a red shawl over her shoulders
And a small book in her lap,
Once in a long while looking up

With the day's brightness on her face,
As if to appraise something of utmost seriousness
She has just read at least twice,

With the sky clear and open to view,
Because the leaves had already fallen
And lay still around her two feet.

Late Train

A few couples walk off into the dark.
In the spot where they vanished,
The trees are swaying as if in a storm
Without making the slightest sound.
The train, too, sits still in the station.

I remember a friend telling me once
How he woke up in a long train
Put out of service in a railroad yard.
In the dining car the tables were all set
With wine glasses and fresh flowers,
And the moon's white glove on one of them.

Here, there's nothing but night and darkness.
In the empty coach, far in the back,
I think I can see one shadowy passenger
Raising his pale hand to wave to me,
Or to peer at the watch on his wrist
I suspect has stopped running years ago.

Sunset's Coloring Book

The blue trees are arguing with the red wind.

The white mare has a peacock for a servant.

The hawk brings the night in its claws.

The golden mountain doesn't exist.

The golden mountain touches the black sky.

Club Midnight

Are you the sole owner of a seedy nightclub?

Are you its sole customer, sole bartender,
Sole waiter prowling around the empty tables?

Do you put on wee-hour girlie shows
With dead stars of black-and-white films?

Is your office upstairs over the neon lights,
Or down deep in the dank rat cellar?

Are bearded Russian thinkers your silent partners?
Do you have a doorman by the name of Dostoyevsky?

Is Fu Manchu coming tonight?
Is Miss Emily Dickinson?

Do you happen to have an immortal soul?
Do you have a sneaky suspicion that you have none?

Is that why you throw a white pair of dice,
In the dark, long after the joint closes?

Late Call

A message for you,
Piece of shit:

You double-crossed us.
You were supposed to
Get yourself crucified
For the sake of the Truth . . .

Who? Me?

The smallest bread crumb
Thankfully overlooked on the dinner table.
A born coward.
A perfect nobody.

And now this!

In the windowpane,
My mouth gutted open.
Aghast.
My judges all wearing black hoods.

It must be a joke.
A big misunderstanding, fellows.
A wrong number, surely?
Someone else's dark night of the soul.

Against Winter

The truth is dark under your eyelids.
What are you going to do about it?
The birds are silent; there's no one to ask.
All day long you'll squint at the gray sky.
When the wind blows you'll shiver like straw.

A meek little lamb, you grew your wool
Till they came after you with huge shears.
Flies hovered over your open mouth,
Then they, too, flew off like the leaves,
The bare branches reached after them in vain.

Winter coming. Like the last heroic soldier
Of a defeated army, you'll stay at your post,
Head bared to the first snowflake.
Till a neighbor comes to yell at you,
You're crazier than the weather, Charlie.

The Emperor

Wears a smirk on his face.
Sits in a wheelchair.
A black cigarillo in one hand,
A live fly in the other.

Hey, sweet mama, he shouts.
I'm wearing my paper crown today
And my wraparound shades
Just for you!

The Garden of Eden parking lot
Needs weeding,
And the candy store
Is now padlocked.

On the street of Elvis look-alikes,
I saw the Klan Wizard in his robes.
I saw the panhandling Jesus
And heard the wind-chime in his head.

It's live horror-movie time,
Says the Emperor,
A can of bug spray in his hand.
He lets my frail mother
Help him cross the street.

She's charmed by his manner and exclaims:
"Such a nice boy!"
Even with his empty eye sockets
And his amputated legs.

When midnight comes —
Commands the Emperor —
Put a mike up to the first roach
Crawling up the kitchen wall.

Let's hear about their exotic dancers,
Their tuxedos-for-rent places,
And see if their witch trials
Are just like the ones we have.

The priest with a flycatcher
On the altar of a church.
The child left as a baby in a shoebox
Now having a haircut in a barbershop.

The Emperor and his three-legged dog
Peeking in through the open door.

■

Make us see what you see in your head,
Emperor.

I see toy soldiers under everyone's feet.
I see a house of cards about to fall.
I see a parrot in a cage admiring himself in a mirror.
I see a tall ladder meant to reach the moon
    teeming with demons and men.

VIII

from Jackstraws

The Voice at 3 A.M.

Who put canned laughter
Into my crucifixion scene?

The Soul Has Many Brides

In India I was greatly taken up
With a fly in a temple
Which gave me the distinct feeling,
It was possible, just possible,
That we had met before.

Was it in Mexico City?
Climbing the blood-spotted, yellow legs
Of the crucified Christ
While his eyes grew larger and larger.
"May God seat you on the highest throne
Of his invisible Kingdom,"
A blind beggar said to me in English.
He knew what I saw.

At the saloon where Pancho Villa
Fired his revolvers at the ceiling,
On the bare ass of a naked nymph
Stepping out of a lake in a painting,
And now shamelessly crawling up
One of Buddha's nostrils,
Whose smile got even more secretive,
Even more squint-eyed.

The Common Insects of North America

Bumble Bee, Soldier Bug, Mormon Cricket,
They are all there somewhere
Behind Joe's Garage, in the tall weeds
By the snake handler's church,
On the fringe of a beaver pond.

Painted Beauty is barefoot and wears shades.
Clouded Wood Nymph has been sightseeing
And has caught a shiver. Book louse
Is reading a book about the battle of Gettysburg.
Chinese Mantid has climbed a leaf to pray.

Hermit Beetle and Rat Flea are feeling amorous
And are going to the drive-in movie.
Widow Dragonfly doing splits in the yard
Could use some serious talking to by her children
Before she comes to a tragic end.

De Occulta Philosophia

Evening sunlight,
Your humble servant
Seeks initiation
Into your occult ways.

Out of the late-summer sky,
Its deepening quiet,
You brought me a summons,
A small share in some large
And obscure knowledge.

Tell me something of your study
Of lengthening shadows,
The blazing windowpanes
Where the soul is turned into light —
Or don't just now.

You have the air of someone
Who prefers to dwell in solitude,
The one who enters, with gravity
Of mien and imposing severity,
A room suddenly rich in enigmas.

O supreme unknowable,
The seemingly inviolable reserve
Of your stratagems
Makes me quake at the thought
Of you finding me thus

Seated in a shadowy back room
At the edge of a village
Bloodied by the setting sun,
To tell me so much,
To tell me absolutely nothing.

Mother Tongue

That's the one the butcher
Wraps in a newspaper
And throws on the rusty scale
Before you take it home

Where a black cat will leap
Off the cold stove
Licking its whiskers
At the sound of her name.

El libro de la sexualidad

The pages of all the books are blank.
The late-night readers at the town library
Make no complaints about that.
They lift their heads solely
To consult the sign commanding silence,
Before they lick their finger,
Look sly, appear to be dozing off,
As they pinch the corner of the paper
Ever so carefully,
While turning the heavy page.

In the yellow puddle of light,
Under the lamp with green shade,
The star charts are all white
In the big astronomy atlas
Lying open between my bare arms.
At the checkout desk, the young Betelgeuse
Is painting her lips red
Using my sweating forehead as a mirror.
Her roving tongue
Is a long-tailed comet in the night sky.

Mummy's Curse

Befriending an eccentric young woman
The sole resident of a secluded Victorian mansion.
She takes long walks in the evening rain,
And so do I, with my hair full of dead leaves.

In her former life, she was an opera singer.
She remembers the rich Neapolitan pastries,
Points to a bit of fresh whipped cream
Still left in the corner of her lower lip,
Tells me she dragged a wooden cross once
Through a leper town somewhere in India.

I was born in Copenhagen, I confide in turn.
My father was a successful mortician.
My mother never lifted her nose out of a book.
Arthur Schopenhauer ruined our happy home.
Since then, a day doesn't go by without me
Sticking a loaded revolver inside my mouth.

She had walked ahead of me and had turned
Like a lion tamer, towering with a whip in hand.
Luckily, in that moment, the mummy sped by
On a bicycle carrying someone's pizza order
And cursing the mist and the potholes.

In the Street

He was kneeling down to tie his shoes, which she mistook for a
    proposal of marriage.
—Arise, arise, sweet man, she said with tears glistening in her
    eyes while people hurried past them as if stung by bees.
—We shall spend the day riding in a balloon, she announced
    happily.
—My ears will pop, he objected.
—We'll throw our clothes overboard as we rise higher and
    higher.
—My cigar that may sputter and cause fireworks.
—Don't worry, my love—she hugged him—even where the
    clouds are darkest, I have a secret getaway.

Filthy Landscape

The season of lurid wildflowers
Sprawled shamelessly over the meadows,
Drunk with necking and kissing
Every hot breeze that comes along.

A small stream opens its legs
In the half-undressed orchard
Teeming with foulmouthed birds
And swarms of smutty fruit flies

In scandalous view of a hilltop
Wrapped in pink clouds of debauchery.
The sun peeking between them,
Now and then like a whoremaster.

Prison Guards Silhouetted Against the Sky

I never gave them a thought. Years had gone by.
Many years. I had plenty of other things
To worry about. Today I was in the dentist's chair
When his new assistant walked in
Pretending not to recognize me in the slightest
As I opened my mouth most obediently.

We were necking in some bushes by the riverbank,
And I wanted her to slip off her bra.
The sky was darkening, there was thunder
When she finally did, so that the first large
Raindrop wet one of her brown nipples.

That was nicer than what she did to my mouth now,
While I winced, while I waited for a wink,
A burst of laughter at the memory of the two of us
Buttoning ourselves, running drenched
Past the state prison with its armed guards
Silhouetted in their towers against the sky.

Jackstraws

My shadow and your shadow on the wall
Caught with arms raised
In display of exaggerated alarm,
Now that even a whisper, even a breath
Will upset the remaining straws
Still standing on the table

In the circle of yellow lamplight,
These few roof beams and columns
Of what could be a Mogul Emperor's palace.
The Prince chews his long nails,
The Princess lowers her green eyelids.
They both smoke too much,
Never go to bed before daybreak.

School for Visionaries

The teacher sits with eyes closed.
When you play chess alone it's always your move.
I'm in the last row with a firefly in the palm of my hand.
The girl with red braids, who saw the girl with red braids?

■

Do you believe in something truer than truth?
Do you prick your ears even when you know damn well no one
    is coming?
Does that explain the lines on your forehead?
Your invisible friend, what happened to her?

■

The rushing wind slides to a stop to listen.
The prisoner opens the thick dictionary lying on his knees.
The floor is cold and his feet are bare.
A chew toy of the gods, is that him?

Do you stare and stare at every black windowpane
As if it were a photo of your unsmiling parents?
Are you homesick for the house of cards?
The sad late-night cough, is it yours?

Ambiguity's Wedding

for E. D.

Bride of Awe, all that's left for us
Are vestiges of a feast table,
Levitating champagne glasses
In the hands of the erased millions.

Mr. So-and-So, the bridegroom
Of absent looks, lost looks,
The pale reporter from the awful doors
Before our identity was leased.

At night's delicious close,
A few avatars of mystery still about,
The spider at his trade,
The print of his vermilion foot on my hand.

A faded woman in sallow dress
Gravely smudged, her shadow on the wall
Becoming visible, a wintry shadow

Quieter than sleep.

Soul, take thy risk.
There where your words and thoughts
Come to a stop,
Encipher me thus, in marriage.

Ancient Divinities

They dish out the usual excuses to one another:
Don't forget, darling, we saw it coming.
The new rationality inspired by geometry
Was going to do us in eventually. Being immortal
Was not worth the price we paid in ridicule.

I feel like I've been wearing a cowbell
Around my neck for two thousand years,
Says one with a shoulder-length blond wig
Raising a champagne glass to her lips
And acknowledging me at the next table,

While at her elbow, next to a napkin
Bloodied by her lipstick, I saw a fly crawling
Out of her overflowing ashtray
Like some poor Trojan or Greek soldier
Who's had enough of wars and their poets.

Obscurely Occupied

You are the Lord of the maimed,
The one bled and crucified
In a cellar of some prison
Over which the day is breaking.

You inspect the latest refinements
Of cruelty. You may even kneel
Down in wonder. They know
Their business, these grim fellows

Whose wives and mothers rise
For the early Mass. You, yourself,
Must hurry back through the snow
Before they find your rightful

Place on the cross vacated,
The few candles burning higher
In your terrifying absence
Under the darkly magnified dome.

Head of a Doll

Whose demon are you,
Whose god? I asked
Of the painted mouth
Half buried in the sand.

A brooding gull
Made a brief assessment,
And tiptoed away
Nodding to himself.

At dusk a firefly or two
Dowsed its eye pits.
And later, toward midnight,
I even heard mice.

On the Meadow

With the wind gusting so wildly,
So unpredictably,
I'm willing to bet one or two ants
May have tumbled on their backs
As we sit here on the porch.

Their feet are pedaling
Imaginary bicycles.
It's a battle of wits against
Various physical laws,
Plus Fate, plus—
So-what-else-is-new?

Wondering if anyone's coming to their aid
Bringing cake crumbs,
Miniature editions of the Bible,
A lost thread or two
Cleverly tied end to end.

Empty Rocking Chair

Talking to yourself on the front porch
As the night blew in
Cold and starless.

Everybody's in harm's way,
I heard you say,
While a caterpillar squirmed
And oozed a pool of black liquid
At your feet.

You turned that notion
Over and over
Until your false teeth
Clamped shut.

Three Photographs

I could've been that kid
In the old high school photograph
I found in a junk shop,
His guileless face circled in black.

In another, there was a view of Brooklyn Bridge
And a tenement roof with pigeons flying
And boys with long poles
Reaching after them into the stormy sky.

In the third, I saw an old man kneeling
With a mouth full of pins
Before a tall, headless woman in white.

I had no money and it was closing time.
I was feeling my way uncertainly
Toward the exit in the evening darkness.

The Toy

The brightly painted horse
Had a boy's face,
And four small wheels
Under his feet,

Plus a long string
To pull him this way and that
Across the floor,
Should you care to.

A string in waiting
That slipped away
With many wiles
From each and every try.

Knock and they'll answer,
My mother told me,
So I climbed the four flights
And went in unannounced.

And found the small toy horse
For the taking.

In the ensuing emptiness
And the fading daylight
That still gives me a shudder
As if I held in my hand
The key to mysteries.

■

Where is the Lost and Found
And the quiet entry,
The undeveloped film
Of the few clear moments
Of our blurred lives?

Where's the drop of blood
And the tiny nail
That pricked my finger
As I bent down to touch the toy,
And caught its eye?

■

Wintry light,
My memories are
Steep stairwells
In dusty buildings
On dead-end streets,

Where I talk to the walls
And closed doors
As if they understood me.

■

The wooden toy sitting pretty.

No quieter than that.

Like the sound of eyebrows
Raised by a villain
In a silent movie.

Psst, someone said behind my back.

Talking to the Ceiling

1

The moths rustle the pages of evening papers.

A beautiful sleepwalker terrorizes a small town in Kansas.

I was snooping on myself, pointing a long finger.

In my youth, boys used to light farts in the dark.

Whose angel wings are that? the cop asked me.

If only I had the instruments for a one-man band

I'd keep the Grim Reaper laughing all the way home.

Oh to press a chimney to my heart on a night like this!

2

Madame Zaza, come to think of it, stays open late.

Go ahead and cut the cards with your eyes closed.

Hangman's convention: ropemaker's workshop.

A hundred horror films were playing in my head.

Mister, would these shoes look good in my coffin? I asked.

Next time, I'll go beddie-bye on a ghost ship.

Next time, I'll befriend a few thimbleweeds

And roll across the Nevada desert as the sun sets.

3

Small-beer metaphysician, king of birdshit,

Coming down from the trees was our first mistake.

The insomniac's brain is a choo-choo train

Dodging sleep like a master criminal was my only talent.

As for Virginia and her new red bikini,

I hear she's been made the official match vendor

Of my dark night of the soul.

Unknown namesake in a roach hotel, go to sleep.

4

And whose exactly are these whispers in my ear?

The colonel on TV praised the use of torture.

He had a pair of eyes I once saw on a dragon riding

The merry-go-round in Texas with a bunch of kids!

The air is sultry, ice melts in a glass alongside a dead fly!

Is that Jesus turning up scared at my bedroom door

Asking to sleep in my old dog's bed?

Selling sticks of gum door-to-door will be all our fate.

5

When I toss and turn and bump my head against the wall

I'm the first to profusely apologize.

That's the way I've been brought up.

On the gallows, with a noose around my neck,

I'll pass out cookies my mother made,

Lift the lid of my coffin to tip the gravediggers,

All because some girl thumbed her nose at me once.

O memory, making me get out to push the hearse!

6

There must be millions of zeros crowding for warmth

Inside my head and making it heavy.

St. John of the Cross and Blaise Pascal coming

With a pair of scales to check for themselves.

Every day, gents, I'm discovering serious new obstacles

To my guaranteed pursuit of happiness.

Naked truth you ought to see the boobs on her!

Here, throw my hat into the lion's cage, I said.

7

What could be causing all this, Doctor?

The old blues, the kind you never lose.

I'm not just any flea on your ass,

I told God apropos of nothing earlier this evening.

Your future is your past, the rain sang softly

Like a scratchy record left to skip on a turntable.

Clock on the wall, have you at least once

Taken a sip of the wine eternity drinks?

Mystic Life

for Charles Wright

It's like fishing in the dark.
Our thoughts are the hooks,
Our hearts the raw bait.

We cast the line past all believing
Into the night sky
Until it's lost to sight.

The line's long unraveling
Rising in our throats like a sigh.

■

One little thought
Leaping into the unthinkable,

Waving an imaginary saber,
Or perhaps a white flag?

The fly and the spider on the ceiling
Looking on in disbelief.

■

It takes a tiny nibble
From time to time
And sends a shiver
Down our spines.

Like hell it does!

■

Say it in your prayers:

In that thou has sought me,
Thou has already found me.

That's what the leaves in the trees
Are all excited about tonight.

■

Solitary fishermen
Lining up like zeros

To infinity.

Therein the mystery
And the pity.

■

The hook left dangling
In the abyss.

Nevertheless, aloft,

White shirttails and all —

I'll be damned!

IX

from Night Picnic

Past-Lives Therapy

They showed me a dashing officer on horseback
Riding past a burning farmhouse
And a barefoot woman in a torn nightgown
Throwing rocks at him and calling him Lucifer,

Explained to me the cause of bloody bandages
I kept seeing in a recurring dream,
Cured the backache I acquired bowing to my old master,
Made me stop putting thumbtacks round my bed.

When I was a straw-headed boy in patched overalls,
Chickens would freely roost in my hair.
Some laid eggs as I played my ukulele
And my mother and father crossed themselves.

Next, I saw myself in an abandoned gas station
Trying to convert a coffin into a spaceship,
Hoarding dead watches in a house in San Francisco,
Spraying obscenities on a highway overpass.

Some days, however, they opened door after door,
Always to a different room, and could not find me.
There'd be a small squeak now and then in the dark,
As if a miner's canary just got caught in a mousetrap.

Couple at Coney Island

It was early one Sunday morning,
So we put on our best rags
And went for a stroll along the boardwalk
Till we came to a kind of palace
With turrets and pennants flying.
It made me think of a wedding cake
In the window of a fancy bakery shop.

I was warm, so I took my jacket off
And put my arm round your waist
And drew you closer to me
While you leaned your head on my shoulder.
Anyone could see we'd made love
The night before and were still giddy on our feet.
We looked naked in our clothes

Staring at the red and white pennants
Whipped by the sea wind.
The rides and shooting galleries
With their ducks marching in line
Still boarded up and padlocked.
No one around yet to take our first dime.

Unmade Beds

They like shady rooms,
Peeling wallpaper,
Cracks on the ceiling,
Flies on the pillow.

If you are tempted to lie down,
Don't be surprised,
You won't mind the dirty sheets,
The rasp of rusty springs
As you make yourself comfy.
The room is a darkened movie theater
Where a grainy
Black-and-white film is being shown.

A blur of disrobed bodies
In the moment of sweet indolence
That follows lovemaking,
When the meanest of hearts
Comes to believe
Happiness can last forever.

Sunday Papers

The butchery of the innocent
Never stops. That's about all
We can ever be sure of, love,
Even more sure than of the roast
You are bringing out of the oven.

It's Sunday. The congregation
Files slowly out of the church
Across the street. A good many
Carry Bibles in their hands.
It's the vague desire for truth
And the mighty fear of it
That make them turn up
Despite the glorious spring weather.

In the hallway, the old mutt
Just now had the honesty
To growl at his own image in the mirror,
Before lumbering off to the kitchen
Where the lamb roast sat
In your outstretched hands
Smelling of garlic and rosemary.

Cherry Blossom Time

Gray sewage bubbling up out of street sewers
After the spring rain with the clear view
Of hawkers of quack remedies and their customers
Swarming on the Capitol steps.

At the National Gallery the saints' tormented faces
Suddenly made sense.
Several turned their eyes on me
As I stepped over the shiny parquetry.

And who and what was I, if you please?
A minor provincial grumbler on a holiday,
With hands clasped behind his back
Nodding to every stranger he meets

As if this were a 1950s Fall of the Roman Empire movie set,
And we the bewildered,
Absurdly costumed, milling extras
Among the pink cherry blossoms.

People Eating Lunch

And thinking with each mouthful,
Or so it appears, seated as they are
At the coffee shop counter, biting
Into thick sandwiches, chewing
And deliberating carefully before taking
Another small sip of their sodas.

The gray-haired counterman
Taking an order has stopped to think
With a pencil paused over his pad,
The fellow in a blue baseball cap
And the woman wearing dark glasses
Are both thoroughly baffled
As they stir and stir their coffees.

If they should look up, they may see
Socrates himself bending over the grill
In a stained white apron and a hat
Made out of yesterday's newspaper,
Tossing an omelet philosophically,
In a small frying pan blackened with fire.

The One to Worry About

I failed miserably at imagining nothing.
Something always came to keep me company:
A small nameless bug crossing the table,
The memory of my mother, the ringing in my ear.
I was distracted and perplexed.
A hole is invariably a hole in something.

About seven this morning, a lone beggar
Waited for me with his small, sickly dog
Whose eyes grew bigger on seeing me.
There goes, the eyes said, that nice man
To whom (appearances to the contrary)
Nothing in this whole wide world is sacred.

I was still a trifle upset entering the bakery
When an unknown woman stepped out
Of the back to wait on me dressed for a night
On the town in a low-cut, tight-fitting black dress.
Her face was solemn, her eyes averted,
While she placed a muffin in my hand,
As if all along she knew what I was thinking.

The Improbable

There may be words left
On the blackboard
In that gray schoolhouse
Shut for the winter break.

Someone was called upon
To wipe them off
And then the bell rang,
The eraser stayed where it was
Next to the chalk.

None of them knew
You'd be passing by this morning
With your eyes raised
As if recollecting
With a thrill of apprehension

Something improbable
That alone makes us possible
As it makes you possible
In this fleeting moment
Before the lights change.

My Father Attributed Immortality to Waiters

for Derek Walcott

For surely, there's no difficulty in understanding
The unreality of an occasional customer
Such as ourselves seated at one of the many tables
As pale as the cloth that covers them.

Time in its augmentations and diminutions,
Does not concern these two in the least.
They stand side by side facing the street,
Wearing identical white jackets and fixed smiles,

Ready to incline their heads in welcome
Should one of us come through the door
After reading the high-priced menu on this street
Of many hunched figures and raised collars.

The Altar

The plastic statue of the Virgin
On top of a bedroom dresser
With a blackened mirror
From a bad-dream grooming salon.

Two pebbles from the grave of a rock star,
A small, grinning wind-up monkey,
A bronze Egyptian coin
And a red movie-ticket stub.

A splotch of sunlight on the framed
Communion photograph of a boy
With the eyes of someone
Who will drown in a lake real soon.

An altar dignifying the god of chance.
What is beautiful, it cautions,
Is found accidentally and not sought after.
What is beautiful is easily lost.

And Then I Think

I'm just a storefront dentist
Extracting a blackened tooth at midnight.

I chewed on many bitter truths, Doc,
My patient says after he spits the blood out

Still slumped over, gray-haired
And smelling of carrion like me.

Of course, I may be the only one here,
And this is a mirror trick I'm performing.

Even the few small crumpled bills
He leaves on the way out, I don't believe in.

I may pluck them with a pair of wet pincers
And count them, and then I may not.

Views from a Train

Then there's aesthetic paradox
Which notes that someone else's tragedy
Often strikes the casual viewer
With the feeling of happiness.

There was the sight of squatters' shacks,
Naked children and lean dogs running
On what looked like a town dump,
The smallest one hopping after them on crutches.

All of a sudden we were in a tunnel.
The wheels ground our thoughts
Back and forth as if they were gravel.
Before long we found ourselves on a beach,
The water blue, the sky cloudless.

Seaside villas, palm trees, white sand;
A woman in a red bikini waved to us
As if she knew each one of us
Individually and was sorry to see us
Heading so quickly into another tunnel.

Icarus's Dog

He let the whole world know
What he thought of his master's stunt.
People threw rocks at him,
But he went on barking.

A hot day's listlessness
Spread over the sea and the sky.
Not even a single gull
To commemorate the event.

Finally, he called it quits and went
To sniff around some bushes,
Vanishing for a moment,
Then reappearing somewhere else,

Wagging his tail happily as he went
Down the long, sandy beach,
Now and then stopping to pee
And take one more look at the sky.

Book Lice

Munching on pages edged in gold
In dust-covered Gideon Bibles
With their tales of God's wrath
And punishment for the wicked
In musty drawers of slummy motels,

While the thin-legged suicide
Draws a steaming bath with a razor in hand,
And the gray-haired car thief
Presses his face on the windowpane
Pockmarked with evening rain.

Three Doors

This one kept its dignity
Despite being kicked
And smudged with hands.

Now the whole neighborhood
Can see what went on last night.
Someone wanted to get in

Real bad and kept pounding
With clenched fists,
Asking God to be his witness.

■

This door's hinges
Give off a nasty squeak
To alert the neighbors.

Some fellow with an
It-pays-to-be-cagey look on his face
Just snuck out.

Yelps of a kicked dog
And wild laughter
Followed after him.

■

I heard a screen door
Creak open at daybreak
And what sounded like stage whisper
While someone let the cat in

Where it rubbed itself
Against two bare legs
And then went and took its first lick
From a saucer of milk.

For the Very Soul of Me

At the close of a sweltering night,
I found him at the entrance
Of a bank building made of blue glass,
Crumpled on his side, naked,
Shielding his crotch with both hands,

The missing one, missed by no one,
As all the truly destitute are,
His rags rolled up into a pillow,
His mouth open as if he were dead,
Or recalling some debauchery.

Insomnia and the heat drove me out early,
Made me turn down one street
Instead of another and saw him
Stretched there, crusted with dirt,
His feet bruised and swollen.

The lone yellow cab idled at the light
With windows down, the sleepy driver
Threw him a glance, shook his head
And drove down the deserted avenue
The rising sun had made beautiful.

Car Graveyard

This is where all our joyrides ended:
Our fathers at the wheel, our mothers
With picnic baskets on their knees
As we sat in the back with our mouths open.

We were driving straight into the sunrise.
The country was flat. A city rose before us,
Its windows burning with the setting sun.
All that vanished as we quit the highway
And rolled down a dusky meadow
Strewn with beer cans and candy wrappers,
Till we came to a stop right here.

First the radio preacher lost his voice,
Then our four tires went flat.
The springs popped out of the upholstery
Like a nest of rattlesnakes
As we tried to remain calm.
Later that night we heard giggles
Out of a junked hearse — then, not a peep
Till the day of the Resurrection.

Wooden Church

It's just a boarded-up shack with a steeple
Under the blazing summer sky
On a back road seldom traveled
Where the shadows of tall trees
Graze peacefully like a row of gallows,
And crows with no carrion in sight
Caw to each other of better days.

The congregation may still be at prayer.
Farm folk from flyspecked photos
Standing in rows with their heads bowed
As if listening to your approaching steps.
So slow they are, they must be asking themselves
How come we are here one minute
And in the very next gone forever?

Try the locked door, then knock once.
The crows will stay out of sight.
High above you, there is the leaning spire
Still feeling the blow of the last storm.
And then the silence of the afternoon . . .
Even the unbeliever must feel its force.

In Praise of Worms

I only have faith in you, Mr. Worm.
You are efficient and dependable
As you go about your grim business.
There's a carcass of a dead cat
Waiting for you in a roadside ditch,

And cries from an outdoor birthday party
As one young girl spins and falls
With a blindfold over her eyes
Underneath some trees festooned
With pennants and Chinese lanterns.

A stroke of lightning and a few raindrops
Is all it took to make them run indoors
And restore the peace in their yard,
So you could take cover under a leaf
And go over your appointment book,

Cross out a name here and there,
Ponder an address or two and set out
In your slow way to pay someone a visit
Among the rich scents of summer night
And the sky brimming with stars.

The Lives of the Alchemists

The great labor was always to efface oneself,
Reappear as something entirely different:
The pillow of a young woman in love,
A ball of lint pretending to be a spider.

Black boredoms of rainy country nights
Thumbing the writings of illustrious adepts
Offering advice on how to proceed with the transmutation
Of a figment of time into eternity.
The true master, one of them counseled,
Needs a hundred years to perfect his art.

In the meantime, the small arcana of the frying pan,
The smell of olive oil and garlic wafting
From room to empty room, the black cat
Rubbing herself against your bare leg
While you shuffle toward the distant light
And the tinkle of glasses in the kitchen.

X

from My Noiseless Entourage

Description of a Lost Thing

It never had a name,
Nor do I remember how I found it.
I carried it in my pocket
Like a lost button
Except it wasn't a button.

Horror movies,
All-night cafeterias,
Dark barrooms
And poolhalls,
On rain-slicked streets.

It led a quiet, unremarkable existence
Like a shadow in a dream,
An angel on a pin,
And then it vanished.
The years passed with their row

Of nameless stations,
Till somebody told me *this is it!*
And fool that I was,
I got off on an empty platform
With no town in sight.

Self-Portrait in Bed

For imaginary visitors, I had a chair
Made of cane I found in the trash.
There was a hole where its seat was
And its legs were wobbly
But it still gave a dignified appearance.

I myself never sat in it, though
With the help of a pillow one could do that
Carefully, with knees drawn together
The way she did once,
Leaning back to laugh at her discomfort.

The lamp on the night table
Did what it could to bestow
An air of mystery to the room.
There was a mirror, too, that made
Everything waver as in a fishbowl

If I happened to look that way,
Red-nosed, about to sneeze,
With a thick wool cap pulled over my ears,
Reading some Russian in bed,
Worrying about my soul, I'm sure.

To Dreams

I'm still living at all the old addresses,
Wearing dark glasses even indoors,
On the hush-hush sharing my bed
With phantoms, visiting the kitchen

After midnight to check the faucet.
I'm late for school, and when I get there
No one seems to recognize me.
I sit disowned, sequestered and withdrawn.

These small shops open only at night
Where I make my unobtrusive purchases,
These back-door movie houses in seedy neighborhoods
Still showing grainy films of my life.

The hero always full of extravagant hope
Losing it all in the end? — whatever it was —
Then walking out into the cold, disbelieving light
Waiting close-lipped at the exit.

My Noiseless Entourage

We were never formally introduced.
I had no idea of their number.
It was like a discreet entourage
Of homegrown angels and demons
All of whom I had met before
And had since largely forgotten.

In time of danger, they made themselves scarce.
Where did they all vanish to?
I asked some felon one night
While he held a knife to my throat,
But he was spooked too,
Letting me go without a word.

It was disconcerting, downright frightening
To be reminded of one's solitude,

Like opening a children's book —
With nothing better to do — reading about stars,
How they can afford to spend centuries
Traveling our way on a glint of light.

Used Clothing Store

A large stock of past lives
To rummage through
For the one that fits you
Cleaned and newly pressed,
Yet frayed at the collar.

A dummy dressed in black
Is at the door to serve you.
His eyes won't let you go.
His mustache looks drawn
With a tip of a dead cigar.

Towers of pants are tilting,
As you turn to flee,
Dead men's hats are rolling
On the floor, hurrying
To escort you out the door.

Voyage to Cythera

I'll go to the island of Cythera
On foot, of course,
I'll set out some May evening,

Light as a feather,
There where the goddess is fabled to have risen
Naked from the sea—

I'll jump over a park fence
Right where the lilacs are blooming
And the trees are feverish with new leaves.
The swing I saw in a painting once
Is surely here somewhere?

And so is the one in a long white dress,
With eyes blindfolded
Who gropes her way down a winding path
Among her masked companions
Wearing black capes and carrying daggers.

This is all a dream, fellows,
I'll say after they empty my pockets.
And so are you, my love,
Carrying a Chinese lantern
And running off with my wallet
In the descending darkness.

Used Book Store

Lovers hold hands in never-opened novels.
The page with a recipe for cucumber soup is missing.
A dead man writes of his happy childhood on a farm,
Of riding in a balloon over Lake Erie.

A sudden draft shuts his book in my hand,
While a philosopher asks how is it possible
To maintain the theologically orthodox doctrine
Of eternal punishment of the damned?

Let's see. There may be sand among the pages
Of a travel guide to Egypt or even a dead flea
That once bit the ass of the mysterious Abigail
Who scribbled her name teasingly with an eye pencil.

Battling Grays

Another grim-lipped day coming our way
Like a gray soldier
From the Civil War monument
Footloose on a narrow country road
With few homes lately foreclosed,
Their windows the color of rain puddles
About to freeze, their yards choked
With weeds and rusty cars.

Small hills like mounds of ashes
Of your dead cigar, general,
Standing bewhiskered and surveying
What the light is in no hurry
To fall upon, including, of course,
Your wound, red and bubbling
Like an accordion, as you raise your saber
To threaten the clouds in the sky.

Sunlight

As if you had a message for me . . .
Tell me about the grains of dust
On my night table?
Is any one of them worth your trouble?

Your burglaries leave no thumbprint.
Mine, too, are silent.
I do my best imagining at night,
And you do yours with the help of shadows.

Like conspirators hatching a plot,
They withdrew one by one
Into corners of the room.
Leaving me the sole witness
Of your burning oratory.

If you did say something, I'm none the wiser.
The breakfast finished,
The coffee dregs were unenlightening.
Like a lion cage at feeding time—
The floor at my feet had turned red.

Minds Roaming

My neighbor was telling me
About her blind cat
Who goes out at night—
Goes where? I asked.

Just then my dead mother called me in
To wash my hands
Because supper was on the table:
The little mouse the cat caught.

Talk Radio

"I was lucky to have a Bible with me.
When the space aliens abducted me . . ."

America, I shouted at the radio,
Even at 2 A.M. you are a loony bin!

No, I take it back!
You are a stone angel in the cemetery

Listening to the geese in the sky,
Your eyes blinded by snow.

My Turn to Confess

A dog trying to write a poem on why he barks,
That's me, dear reader!
They were about to kick me out of the library
But I warned them,
My master is invisible and all-powerful.
Still, they kept dragging me out by the tail.

In the park the birds spoke freely of their own vexations.
On a bench, I saw an old woman
Cutting her white curly hair with imaginary scissors
While staring into a small pocket mirror.

I didn't say anything then,
But that night I lay slumped on the floor,
Chewing on a pencil,

Sighing from time to time,
Growling, too, at something out there
I could not bring myself to name.

On the Farm

The cows are to be slaughtered
And the sheep, too, of course.
The same for the hogs sighing in their pens—
And as for the chickens,

Two have been killed for dinner tonight,
While the rest peck side by side
As the shadows lengthen in the yard
And bales of hay turn gold in the fields.

One cow has stopped grazing
And has looked up puzzled
Seeing a little white cloud
Trot off like a calf into the sunset.

On the porch someone has pressed
A rocking chair into service
But we can't tell who it is—a stranger,
Or that boy of ours who never has anything to say?

Snowy Morning Blues

The translator is a close reader.
He wears thick glasses
As he peers out the window
At the snowy fields and bushes
That are like a sheet of paper
Covered with quick scribble
In a language he knows well enough,
Without knowing any words in it,

Only what the eyes discern,
And the heart intuits of its idiom.
So quiet now, not even a faint
Rustle of a page being turned
In a white and wordless dictionary
For the translator to avail himself
Before whatever words are left
Grow obscure in the coming darkness.

To Fate

You were always more real to me than God.
Setting up the props for a tragedy,
Hammering the nails in
With only a few close friends invited to watch.

Just to be neighborly, you made a pretty girl lame,
Ran over a child with a motorcycle.
I can think of many other examples.
Ditto: How the two of us keep meeting.

A fortunetelling gumball machine in Chinatown
May have the answer,
An old creaky door opening in a horror film,
A pack of cards I left on a beach.

I can feel you snuggle close to me at night,
With your hot breath, your cold hands —
And me already like an old piano
Dangling out of a window at the end of a rope.

Sweetest

Little candy in death's candy shop,
I gave your sugar a lick
When no one was looking,
Took you for a ride on my tongue
To all the secret places,

Trying to appear above suspicion
As I went about inspecting the confectionary,
Greeting the owner with a nod
With you safely tucked away
And melting to nothing in my mouth.

The Tragic Sense of Life

Because few here recall the old wars,
The burning of Atlanta and Dresden,
The great-uncle who lies in Arlington,
Or that Vietnam vet on crutches
Who tries to bum a dime or a cigarette.

The lake is still in the early-morning light.
The road winds; I slow down to let
A small, furry animal cross in a hurry.
The few remaining wisps of fog
Are like smoke rising out of cannons.

In one little town flags fly over dark houses.
Outside a church made of gray stone,
The statue of the Virgin blesses the day.
Her son is inside afraid to light a candle,
Saying, *Forgive one another, clothe the naked.*

Niobe and her children may live here.
As for me, I don't know where I am—
And here I'm already leaving in a hurry
Down a stretch of road with little to see,
Dark woods everywhere closing in on me.

In the Planetarium

Never-yet-equaled, wide-screen blockbuster
That grew more and more muddled
After a spectacular opening shot.
The pace, even for the most patient
Killingly slow despite the promise
Of a show-stopping, eye-popping ending:
The sudden shriveling of the whole
To its teensy starting point, erasing all—
Including this bag of popcorn we are sharing.

Yes, an intriguing but finally irritating
Puzzle with no answer forthcoming tonight
From the large cast of stars and galaxies

In what may be called a prodigious
Expenditure of time, money and talent.
"Let's get the fuck out of here," I said
Just as her upraised eyes grew moist
And she confided to me, much too loudly,
"I have never seen anything so beautiful."

The Absentee Landlord

Surely, he could make it easier
When it comes to inquiries
As to his whereabouts.
Rein in our foolish speculations,
Silence our voices raised in anger,

And not leave us alone
With that curious feeling
We sometimes have
Of there being a higher purpose
To our residing here
Where nothing works
And everything needs fixing.

The least he could do is put up a sign:
AWAY ON BUSINESS
So we could see it,
In the graveyard where he collects the rent
Or in the night sky
Where we address our complaints to him.

My Wife Lifts a Finger to Her Lips

Night is coming.
A lone hitchhiker
Holds up a homemade sign.

Masked figures
Around a gambling table?
No, those are scarecrows in a field.

At the neighbors',
Where they adore a black cat,
There's no light yet.

Dear Lord, can you see
The fleas run for cover?
No, he can't see the fleas.

Pigeons at Dawn

Extraordinary efforts are being made
To hide things from us, my friend.
Some stay up into the wee hours
To search their souls.
Others undress each other in darkened rooms.

The creaky old elevator
Took us down to the icy cellar first
To show us a mop and a bucket
Before it deigned to ascend again
With a sigh of exasperation.

Under the vast, early-dawn sky
The city lay silent before us.
Everything on hold:
Rooftops and water towers,
Clouds and wisps of white smoke.

We must be patient, we told ourselves,
See if the pigeons will coo now
For the one who comes to her window
To feed them angel cake,
All but invisible, but for her slender arm.

XI

from That Little Something

Walking

I never run into anyone from the old days.
It's summer and I'm alone in the city.
I enter stores, apartment houses, offices
And find nothing remotely familiar.

The trees in the park — were they always so big?
And the birds so hidden, so quiet?
Where is the bus that passed this way?
Where are the greengrocers and hairdressers,

And that schoolhouse with the red fence?
Miss Harding is probably still at her desk,
Sighing as she grades papers late into the night.
The bummer is, I can't find the street.

All I can do is make another tour of the neighborhood,
Hoping I'll meet someone to show me the way
And a place to sleep, since I've no return ticket
To wherever it is I came from earlier this evening.

That Little Something

for Li-Young Lee

The likelihood of ever finding it is small.
It's like being accosted by a woman
And asked to help her look for a pearl
She lost right here in the street.

She could be making it all up,
Even her tears, you say to yourself,
As you search under your feet,
Thinking, Not in a million years . . .

It's one of those summer afternoons
When one needs a good excuse
To step out of a cool shade.
In the meantime, what ever became of her?

And why, years later, do you still,
Off and on, cast your eyes to the ground
As you hurry to some appointment
Where you are now certain to arrive late?

Night Clerk in a Roach Hotel

I'm the furtive inspector of dimly lit corridors,
Dead lightbulbs and red exit signs,
Doors that show traces
Of numerous attempts at violent entry,

Is that the sound of a maid making a bed at midnight?
The rustle of counterfeit bills
Being counted in the wedding suite?
A fine-tooth comb passing through a head of gray hair?

Eternity is a mirror and a spider web,
Someone wrote with lipstick in the elevator.
I better get the passkey and see for myself.
I better bring along a book of matches too.

Waiting for the Sun to Set

These rows of tall palm trees,
White villas and white hotels
Fronting the beach and the sea
Seem most improbable to me

Whiling away the afternoon
In a cane rocking chair
On a small, secluded veranda,
Overrun with exotic flowers

I don't even know the names of,
Raised as I was by parents
Who kept the curtains drawn,
The lights low, the stove unlit,

Leaving me as wary as they'd be
At first seeing oranges in a tree,
Women running bare-breasted
Over pink sands in a blue dusk.

House of Cards

I miss you winter evenings
With your dim lights.
The shut lips of my mother
And our held breaths
As we sat at a dining room table.

Her long, thin fingers
Stacking the cards,
Then waiting for them to fall.
The sound of boots in the street
Making us still for a moment.

There's no more to tell.
The door is locked,
And in one red-tinted window,
A single tree in the yard,
Stands leafless and misshapen.

Aunt Dinah Sailed to China

Bearded ancestors, what became of you?
Have you gone and hid yourself
In some cabin in the woods
To listen to your whiskers grow in peace?

Clergymen patting chin curtains,
Soldiers with door knockers,
Sickly youths with goatees,
Town drunks proud of their ducktails.

Cousin Kate, was that a real mustache
You wore as you stood in church
Waiting for your bridegroom
To run up the stairs someday?

And you, Grandpa, when you shouted at God
To do something about the world,
He kept quiet and let the night fall,
Seeing that your beard was whiter than his.

To Laziness

Only you understood
How little time we are given,
Not enough to lift a finger.
The voices on the stairs,
Thoughts too quick to pursue,
What do they all matter?
When eternity beckons.

The heavy curtains drawn,
The newspapers unread.
The keys collecting dust.
The flies either sluggish or dead.
The bed like a slow boat,
With its one listless sail
Made of cigarette smoke.

When I did move at last,
The stores were closed.
Was it already Sunday?
The weddings and funerals were over.
The one or two white clouds left
Above the dark rooftops,
Not sure which way to go.

Listen

Everything about you,
My life, is both
Make-believe and real.

We are a couple
Working the night shift
In a bomb factory.

"Come quietly," one says
To the other
As he takes her by the hand
And leads her
To a rooftop
Overlooking the city.

At this hour, if one listens
Long and hard,
One can hear a fire engine
In the distance,
But not the cries for help,

Just the silence
Growing deeper
At the sight of a small child
Leaping out of a window
With its nightclothes on fire.

Encyclopedia of Horror

Nobody reads it but the insomniacs.
How strange to find a child,
Slapped by his mother only this morning,
And the mad homeless woman
Who squatted to urinate in the street.

Perhaps they've missed someone?
That smoke-shrouded city after a bombing raid,
The corpses like cigarette butts
In a dinner plate overflowing with ashes.
But no, everyone is here.

O were you to come, invisible tribunal,
There'd be too many images to thumb through,
Too many stories to listen to,
Like the one about guards playing cards
After they were done beating their prisoner.

Dance of the Macabre Mice

"In the land of turkeys in turkey weather"
— W. STEVENS

The president smiles to himself; he loves war
And another one is coming soon.
Each day we can feel the merriment mount
In government offices and TV studios
As our bombs fall on distant countries.

The mortuaries are being scrubbed clean.
Soon they'll be full of grim young men laid out in rows.
Already the crowd gurgles with delight
At the bird-sweet deceits, the deep-throated lies
About our coming battles and victories.

Dark-clad sharpshooters on rooftops
Are scanning the mall for suspicious pigeons,
Blind men waving their canes in the air,
Girls with short skirts and ample bosoms
Reaching deep into their purses for a lighter.

The Lights Are On Everywhere

The Emperor must not be told night is coming.
His armies are chasing shadows,
Arresting whippoorwills and hermit thrushes
And setting towns and villages on fire.

In the capital, they go around confiscating
Clocks and watches, burning heretics
And painting the sunrise above the rooftops
So we can wish each other good morning.

The rooster brought in chains is crowing,
The flowers in the garden have been forced to stay open,
And still yet dark stains spread over the palace floors
Which no amount of scrubbing will wipe away.

Memories of the Future

There are one or two murderers in any crowd.
They do not suspect their destinies yet.
Wars are started to make it easy for them
To kill that woman pushing a baby carriage.

The animals in the zoo don't hide their worry.
They pace their cages or shy away from us
Listening to something we can't hear yet:
The coffin makers hammering their nails.

The strawberries are already in season
And so are the scallions and radishes.

A young man buys roses, another rides
A bike through the traffic using no hands.

Old fellow bending over the curb to vomit,
Betake thee to thy own place of torment.
The sky at sunset is red with grilling coals.
A thick glove reaches through the fire after us.

In the Junk Store

A small, straw basket
Full of medals
From good old wars
No one recalls.

I flipped one over
To feel the pin
That once pierced
The hero's swelling chest.

Madmen Are Running the World

Watch it spin like a wheel
And get stuck in the mud.

The truck is full of caged chickens
Squawking about their fate.

The driver has gone to get help
In a dive with a live band.

Myrtle, Phyllis, or whatever they call you girls!
Get some shuteye while you can.

In the Afternoon

The devil likes the chicken coop.
He lies on a bed of straw
Watching the snow fall.
The hens fetch him eggs to suck,
But he's not in the mood.

Cotton Mather is coming tonight,
Bringing a young witch.
Her robe already licked by flames,
Her bare feet turning pink
While she steps to the woodpile,

Saying a prayer; her hands
Like mating butterflies,
Or are they snowflakes?
As the smoke rises,
And the gray afternoon light returns

With its wild apple tree
And its blue pickup truck,
The one with a flat tire,
And the rusted kitchen stove
They meant to take to the dump.

Prophesy

The last customer will stagger out of the door.
Cooks will hang their white hats.
Chairs will climb on the tables.
A broom will take a lazy stroll into a closet.

The waiters will kick off their shoes.
The cat will get a whole trout for dinner.
The cashier will stop counting receipts,
Scratch her ass with a pencil and sigh.

The boss will pour himself another brandy.
The mirrors will grow tired of potted palms
And darken slowly the way they always do
When someone runs off with a roast chicken.

A Row of High Windows

Sky's gravedigger,
Bird catcher,
Dark night's match seller—
Or whatever you are?

A book-lined tomb,
Pots and pans music hall,
Insomnia's sick nurse,
Burglar's blind date.

Also you
Stripper's darkened stage
Right next to a holy martyr
Being flayed by the setting sun.

Secret History

Of the light in my room:
Its mood swings,
Dark-morning glooms,
Summer ecstasies.

Spider on the wall,
Lamp burning late,
Shoes left by the bed,
I'm your humble scribe.

Dust balls, simple souls
Conferring in the corner.
The pearl earring she lost,
Still to be found.

Silence of falling snow,
Night vanishing without trace,
Only to return.
I'm your humble scribe.

Wire Hangers

All they need
Is one little red dress
To start swaying
In that empty closet

For the rest of them
To nudge each other,
Clicking like knitting needles
Or disapproving tongues.

Labor and Capital

The softness of this motel bed
On which we made love
Demonstrates to me in an impressive manner
The superiority of capitalism.

At the mattress factory, I imagine,
The employees are happy today.
It's Sunday and they are working
Extra hours, like us, for no pay.

Still, the way you open your legs
And reach for me with your hand
Makes me think of the Revolution,
Red banners, crowd charging.

Someone stepping on a soapbox
As the flames engulf the palace,
And the old prince in full view
Steps to his death from a balcony.

The Bather

Where the path to the lake twists
Out of sight, a puff of dust,
The kind bare feet make running.
A low branch heavy with leaves
Swaying momentarily
In the dense and somber shade.

A late bather disrobing for a dip,
Pinned hair coming undone soon to float
As she flips on her back letting
The sleepy current take her
Over the dark water to where the sky
Opens wide, the night blurring

Her nakedness, the silence thick,
Treetops like charred paper edges,
Even the insects oddly reclusive,
The rare breath of wind in the leaves
Fooling me to look once again,
Until the chill made me rise and go in.

Eternities

Discreet reader of discreet lives.
Chairs no one ever sits in.
Motes of dust, their dancing days done.
Schools of yellow fish
On the peeling wallpaper
Keeping their eyes on you.
It's late for today, late.
A small crucifix over the bed
Watches over a stopped clock.

◼

Sewing room, linty daylight
Through a small window.
You will never be in my shoes, Eternity.
I come with an expiration date.

My scissors cut black cloth.
I stick silver pins into a tailor's dummy,
Muttering some man's name
While aiming at its heart.

■

Raleigh played cards with his executioners.
I sit over a dead mouse in the kitchen.
Hot night, the windows open,
The air rich with the scents of lilacs
And banked fires of backyard grills.
My lovely neighbor must be sleeping naked,
Or lighting a match to see what time it is.

■

The torment of branches in the wind.
Is the sea hearing their confession?
The little white clouds must think so.
They are rushing over to hear.
The ship on the way to paradise
Seems stuck on the horizon,
Pinned by one golden pin of sunlight.
Only the great rocks act as if nothing's the matter.

■

In a city where so much is hidden:
The crimes, the riches, the beautiful women,
You and I were lost for hours.
We went in to ask a butcher for directions.
He sat playing the accordion.

The lambs had their eyes closed in bliss,
But not the knives, his evil little helpers.
Come right in, folks, he said.

■

Conscience, that awful power,
With its vast network of spies,
Secret arrests at night,
Dreaded prisons and reform schools,
Beatings and forced confessions,
Wee-hour crucifixions.
A small, dead bird in my hand
Is all the evidence they had.

■

The sprawling meadow bordered by a stream,
Naked girl on horseback.
Yes, I do remember that.
Sunlight on the outhouse wall,
One little tree in the yard afraid of darkness,
The voice of the hermit thrush.

■

Thoughts frightened of the light,
Frightened of each other.
They listen to a clock ticking.
Like flock of sheep led to slaughter,
The seconds keep a good pace,

Stick together, don't look back,
All worried, as they go,
What their shepherd may be thinking.

■

A sough of wind in the open window
Making the leaves sigh.
"I come to you like one
Who is dying of love,"
God said to Christine Ebner
On this dull, sultry night.
"I come to you with the desire
Of bridegroom for his bride."

■

Soul's jukebox
Playing golden oldies
In the sky
Strewn with stars.
When I ask God
What size coin it takes
I'm greeted
With stunned silence.

Eternity's Orphans

One night you and I were walking.
The moon was so bright
We could see the path under the trees.
Then the clouds came and hid it
So we had to grope our way
Till we felt the sand under our bare feet,
And heard the pounding waves.

Do you remember telling me,
"Everything outside this moment is a lie"?
We were undressing in the dark
Right at the water's edge
When I slipped the watch off my wrist
And without being seen or saying
Anything in reply, I threw it into the sea.

XII

from Master of Disguises

Master of Disguises

Surely, he walks among us unrecognized:
Some barber, store clerk, delivery man,
Pharmacist, hairdresser, bodybuilder,
Exotic dancer, gem cutter, dog walker,
The blind beggar singing, O Lord, remember me,

Some window decorator starting a fake fire
In a fake fireplace while mother and father watch
From the couch with their frozen smiles
As the street empties and the time comes
For the undertaker and the last waiter to head home.

O homeless old man, standing in a doorway
With your face half hidden,
I wouldn't even rule out the black cat crossing the street,
The bare lightbulb swinging on a wire
In a subway tunnel as the train comes to a stop.

Nineteen Thirty-eight

That was the year the Nazis marched into Vienna,
Superman made his debut in Action Comics,
Stalin was killing off his fellow revolutionaries,
The first Dairy Queen opened in Kankakee, Ill.,
As I lay in my crib peeing in my diapers.

"You must've been a beautiful baby," Bing Crosby sang.
A pilot the newspapers called Wrong Way Corrigan

Took off from New York heading for California
And landed instead in Ireland, as I watched my mother
Take a breast out of her blue robe and come closer.

There was a hurricane that September causing a movie theater
At Westhampton Beach to be lifted out to sea.
People worried the world was about to end.
A fish believed to have been extinct for seventy million years
Came up in a fishing net off the coast of South Africa.

I lay in my crib as the days got shorter and colder,
And the first heavy snow fell in the night
Making everything very quiet in my room.
I thought I heard myself cry for a long, long time.

Preachers Warn

This peaceful world of ours is ready for destruction—
And still the sun shines, the sparrows come
Each morning to the bakery for crumbs.
Next door, two men deliver a bed for a pair of newlyweds
And stop to admire a bicycle chained to a parking meter.
Its owner is making lunch for his ailing grandmother.
He heats the soup and serves it to her in a bowl.

The windows are open, there's a warm breeze.
The young trees on our street are delirious to have leaves.
Italian opera is on the radio, the volume too high.
Brevi e tristi giorni visse, a baritone sings.
Everyone up and down our block can hear him.
Something about the days that remain for us to enjoy
Being few and sad. Not today, Maestro Verdi!

At the hairdresser's a girl leaps out of a chair,
Her blond hair bouncing off her bare shoulders
As she runs out the door in her high heels.
"I must be off," says the handsome boy to his grandmother.
His bicycle is where he left it.
He rides it casually through the heavy traffic
His white shirttails fluttering behind him
Long after everyone else has come to a sudden stop.

Old Man

Backed myself into a dark corner one day,
Found a boy there
Forgotten by teachers and classmates,
His shoulders slumped,
The hair on his head already gray.
Friend, I said.

While you stood here staring at the wall,
They shot a president,
Some guy walked on the moon,
Dolly, the girl we all loved,
Took too many sleeping pills and died
In a hotel room in Santa Monica.

Now and then I thought of you,
Listening to the squeak of the chalk
On the blackboard,
The sighs and whispers
Of unknown children
Bent over their lessons,
The mice running in the night.

Visions of unspeakable loveliness
Must've come to you in your misery:
Cloudless skies on long June evenings,
Trees full of cherries in our orchard,
To make you ache and want to be with me,
Driving a cab in New York City.

Nancy Jane

Grandma laughing on her deathbed.
Eternity, the quiet one, listening in.

Like moths around an oil lamp we were.
Like rag dolls tucked away in the attic.

In walked a cat with a mouthful of feathers.
(How about that?)

A dark little country store full of gravediggers' children
    buying candy.
(That's how we looked that night.)

The young man pumping gas spoke of his friends: the clouds.
It was such a sad story, it made everyone laugh.

A bird called out of a tree, but received no answer.

The beauty of that last moment
Like a red sail on the bay at sunset,

Or like a wheel breaking off a car
And roaming the world on its own.

Carrying On Like a Crow

Are you authorized to speak
For these trees without leaves?
Are you able to explain
What the wind intends to do
With a man's shirt and a woman's nightgown
Left on the laundry line?
What do you know about dark clouds?
Ponds full of fallen leaves?
Old-model cars rusting in a driveway?
Who gave you the permission
To look at the beer can in a ditch?
The white cross by the side of the road?
The swing set in the widow's yard?
Ask yourself, if words are enough,
Or if you'd be better off
Flapping your wings from tree to tree
And carrying on like a crow.

Driving Home

Minister of our coming doom, preaching
On the car radio, how right
Your hell and damnation sound to me
As I travel these small, bleak roads
Thinking of the mailman's son
The army sent back in a sealed coffin.

His house is around the next turn.
A forlorn mutt sits in the yard

Waiting for someone to come home.
I can see the TV is on in the living room,
Canned laughter in the empty house
Like the sound of beer cans tied to a hearse.

Sightseeing in the Capital

These grand old buildings
With their spacious conference rooms,
Leather-padded doors,
Where they weigh life and death
Without a moment of fear
Of ever being held accountable,

And then withdraw to dine in style
And drink to each other's health
In private clubs and country estates,
While we linger on the sidewalk
Admiring the rows of windows
The evening sun has struck blind.

Daughters of Memory

There were three of them, always three,
Sunbathing side by side on the beach,
The sound of waves and children's voices so soothing
It was hard to stay awake.

When I woke, the sun was setting.
The three friends knelt in a circle
Taking turns to peek into a small mirror
And comb their hair with the same comb.

Months later, I happened to see two of them
Running in the rain after school,
Ducking into a doorway with a pack of cigarettes
And a glance at me in my new uniform.

In the end, there was just one girl left,
Tall and beautiful,
Making late rounds in a hospital ward,
Past a row of beds, one of which was mine.

In That Big House

When she still knew how to make shadows speak
By sitting with them a long time,
They talked about her handsome father,
His long absence, and how the quiet
Would fill the house on snowy evenings.

"Tell us, child, are you afraid?" they'd ask,
While the girl listened for steps in the hallway,
The long, dim one with a full-length mirror
That's been going blind like her grandmother
Who could no longer find or thread a needle

As she sat in the parlor remembering some actors
Her son brought to dinner one night,
The one young woman who wandered off by herself
And was found later, after a long search,
Floating naked in the black water of the pond.

Puppet Maker

In his fear of solitude, he made us.
Fearing eternity, he gave us time.
I hear his white cane thumping
Up and down the hall.

I expect neighbors to complain, but no.
The little girl who sobbed
When her daddy crawled into her bed
Is quiet now.

It's quarter to two.
On this street of darkened pawnshops,
Welfare hotels and tenements,
One or two ragged puppets are awake.

Summer Storm

I'm going over to see what those weeds
By the stone wall are fretting about.
Perhaps they don't care for the way
The shadows creep across the lawn
In the silence of the afternoon.

The sky keeps being blue,
Though we hear no birds,
See no butterflies among the flowers,
No ants running over our feet.
As for the trees in our yard,

They bend their branches ever so slightly
In deference to something
About to make its entrance
Of which we know nothing,
Spellbound as we are by the deepening quiet.

The Melon

There was a melon fresh from the garden
So ripe the knife slurped
As it cut it into six slices.
The children were going back to school.
Their mother, passing out paper plates,
Would not live to see the leaves fall.

I remember a hornet, too, that flew in
Through the open window
Mad to taste the sweet fruit
While we ducked and screamed,
Covered our heads and faces,
And sat laughing after it was gone.

The Lovers

In the woods one fair Sunday,
When we were children,
We came upon a couple lying on the ground.

Hand in hand, ourselves afraid
Of losing our way, we saw
What we first thought was a patch of snow,

The two clutching each other naked
On the bare ground, the wind
Swaying the branches over them

As we stole by, never to find out
Who they were, never to mention it afterwards
To each other, or to anyone else.

The Empress

My beloved, you who spend your nights
Torturing me
By holding up one mirror after another
To me in the dark,
If there's anything I know to say or do today,
I merit no praise for it,
But owe it to the subtlety of your torments,
And your perseverance in keeping me awake.

All the same, who gave you the right
To judge me in my wretchedness?
What soul white as snow
Compiled this endless list of misdeeds
You read to me every night?
The airs you put on when I tell you to stop
Would make one believe
You were once a bedmate of a Chinese emperor.

I like it best when we do not say a word.
When we lie side by side
Like two lovers after their passion is spent.
Once again, day is breaking.

A small bird in the trees is pouring her heart out
At the miracle of the coming light.
It hurts.
The beauty of a night spent sleepless.

The Toad

It'll be a while before my friends
See me in the city,
A while before we roam the streets
Late at night
Shouting each other's names
To point out some sight too wonderful
Or too terrifying
To give it a name in a hurry.

I'm staying put in the country,
Rising early,
Listening to the birds
Greet the light,
And when they fall quiet,
To the wind in the leaves
Which are as numerous here
As the crowds in your city.

God never made a day as beautiful as today,
A neighbor was saying.
I sat in the shade after she left
Mulling that one over,
When a toad hopped out of the grass
And, finding me harmless,
Hopped over my foot on his way to the pond.

Summer Light

It likes empty churches
At the blue hour of dawn.

The shadows parting
Like curtains in a sideshow,

The eyes of the crucified
Staring down from the cross

As if seeing his bloody feet
For the very first time.

The Invisible

1

It was always here.
Its vast terrors concealed
By this costume party
Of flowers and birds
And children playing in the garden.

Only the leaves tell the truth.
They rustle darkly,
Then fall silent as if listening
To a dragonfly
Who may know a lot more of the invisible,

Or why else would its wings be
So translucent in the light,

So swift to take flight,
One barely notices
It's been here and gone.

2

Don't the shadows know something about it?
The way they, too, come and go
As if paying a visit to that other world
Where they do what they do
Before hurrying back to us.

Just today I was admiring the one I cast
As I walked alone in the street
And was about to engage it in conversation
On this very topic
When it took leave of me suddenly.

Shadow, I said, what message
Will you bring back to me,
And will it be full of dark ambiguities
I can't even begin to imagine
As I make my slow way in the midday sun?

3

It may be hiding behind a door
In some office building,
Where one day you found yourself
After hours
With no one to ask for directions,
Among the hundreds of doors
All lacking information what sort of business,
What sort of drudgery goes on
Inside its narrow, poorly lit rooms.

Some detective agency
That'll find God for a small fee?
Some company ready to insure you,
Should one day,
Despite the promises of your parish priest,
You turn up in hell?

The long hallway ends at a window
Where even the light of the dying day
Seems old and dusty.
It understands what waiting is,
And when found out
Appears surprised to see you here.

4

The moment you shut off the lamp,
Here they are again,
The two dead people
You called your parents.

You'd hoped you'd see tonight
The girl you loved once,
And that other one who let you
Slip a hand under her skirt.

Instead, here's that key in a saucer of small change
That wouldn't open any lock,
The used condom you found in church,
The lame crow your neighbor kept.

Here's the fly you once tortured,
A rock you threw at your best friend,
The pig that let out a scream
As the knife touched its throat.

5

People here still tell stories
About a blind old man
Who rolled dice on the sidewalk
And paid children
In the neighborhood
To tell him what number came up.

When they were away in school,
He'd ask anyone
Whose steps he heard,
The mailman making his rounds,
The undertakers loading a coffin in their black wagon,
And you, too, mister,
Should you happen to come along.

6

Dark evening, gray old tenement,
A white cat in one window,
An old man eating his dinner in another.
Everyone else hidden from view,

Like the one who waits for the tub
To fill up with hot water
While she undresses before a mirror
Already beginning to steam over.

Imagination, devil's helper,
Made me glimpse her two breasts
As I hurried by with my face tucked in my collar,
Because the wind was raw.

7.

Dear Miss Russell:

Nights, you took me on a private tour
Of the empty town library.
I could hardly keep up
As you darted along the rows of books,
Whispering their names,
Pointing out the ones I ought to read,

Then forgetting all about me,
Pulling the light cord
And leaving me in the dark
To grope for a book
Among the shelves,
Surely the wrong one,

As I was soon to learn
At the checkout desk
Under your pitying gaze
That followed me into the street
Where I dared not stop
To see what I held in my hand
Until I had rounded the corner.

8

A rusty key from a cigar box full of keys
In a roadside junk shop.
The one I held on to a long time
Before I let it slip
Through my fingers.

Most likely, when it was still in use,
The reclusive author
Of "The Minister's Black Veil"
Was still cooped up
In his mother's house in Salem.

It opened a small drawer
With a stack of yellowed letters
In a dresser with a mirror
That gave back a pale face
With a pair of feverish eyes

In a room with a view
Of black, leafless trees
And red clouds hurrying at sunset,
Where soon tears fell
Causing the key to go rusty.

9

O Persephone, is it true what they say,
That everything that is beautiful,
Even for one fleeting moment,
Descends to you, never to return?

Dressmaker pinning a red dress in a store window,
Old man walking your sickly old dog,
Even you little children holding hands
As you cross the busy street with your teacher,

What hope do you have for us today?
With the sky darkening so early,
The first arriving flakes of snow,
Falling here and there, then everywhere.

10

Invisible one, watching the snow
Through a dark window
From a row of dark schoolhouse windows,
Making sure the snowflakes fall
In proper order
Where they were fated to fall
In the gray yard,
And hush the moment they do.

The crow nodding his head
As he walks by
Must've been a professor of philosophy
In a previous life
Who despite changed circumstances
Still opens his beak
From time to time
As if to address his adoring students,
And seeing nothing but snow,
Looks up puzzled
At one of the dark windows.

11

Bird comforting the afflicted
With your song,
The one or two lying awake
In the vast slumber
Of small town and countryside,

Who know nothing of each other
As they listen intently
To every little tweet
Afraid they'll do something
To make it hush.

In the cool, silvery light,
The outline of the window visible,
Some trees in the yard
About to let go of the night,
The others in no big hurry.

XIII

from The Voice at 3:00 A.M.

Postcard from S.

So far I've met here two Homers and one Virgil.
The town is like a living anthology of classic literature.
Thunder and lightning almost every afternoon.
When neighbors meet, they slap mosquitoes
On each other's foreheads and go off red in the face.

I'm lying in a hammock next to a burning barn
Watching a birch tree in the yard.
One minute it wrestles with the wind and smoke,
The next it raises its fists to curse the gods.
That, of course, makes it a Trojan
To the Greeks just arriving on a fire engine.

Empty Barbershop

In pursuit of happiness, you may yet
Draw close to it momentarily
In one of these two leather-bound chairs
With the help of scissors and a comb,

Draped to the chin with a long white sheet,
While your head slips through
The invisible barber's greasy fingers
Making your hair stand up straight,

While he presses the razor to your throat,
Causing your eyes to spring open
As you discern in the mirror before you
The full length of the empty barbershop

With two vacant chairs and past them
The street, commensurately empty,
Except for the pressed and blurred face
Of someone straining to look inside.

Grayheaded Schoolchildren

Old men have bad dreams,
So they sleep little.
They walk on bare feet
Without turning on the lights,
Or they stand leaning
On gloomy furniture
Listening to their hearts beat.

The one window across the room
Is black like a blackboard.
Every old man is alone
In this classroom, squinting
At that fine chalk line
That divides being-here
From being-here-no-more.

No matter. It was a glass of water
They were going to get,
But not just yet.
They listen for mice in the walls,
A car passing on the street,
Their dead fathers shuffling past them
On their way to the kitchen.

Serving Time

Another dreary day in time's invisible
Penitentiary, making license plates
With lots of zeros, walking lockstep counter-
clockwise in the exercise yard or watching
The lights dim when some poor fellow,
Who could as well be me, gets fried.

Here on death row, I read a lot of books.
First it was law, as you'd expect.
Then came history, ancient and modern.
Finally philosophy — all that being-and-nothingness stuff.
The more I read, the less I understand.
Still, other inmates call me professor.

Did I mention that we had no guards?
It's a closed book who locks
And unlocks the cell doors for us.
Even the executions we carry out
By ourselves, attaching the wires,
Playing warden, playing chaplain

All because a little voice in our head
Whispers something about our last appeal
Being denied by God himself.
The others hear nothing, of course,
But that, typically, you may as well face it,
Is how time runs things around here.

Autumn Sky

In my great-grandmother's time,
All one needed was a broom
To get to see places
And give the geese a chase in the sky.

∎

The stars know everything,
So we try to read their minds.
As distant as they are,
We choose to whisper in their presence.

∎

Oh, Cynthia,
Take a clock that has lost its hands
For a ride.
Get me a room at Hotel Eternity
Where Time likes to stop now and then.

∎

Come, lovers of dark corners,
The sky says,
And sit in one of my dark corners.
There are tasty little zeros
In the peanut dish tonight.

Separate Truths

Night fell without asking
For our permission.
Mary had a headache,
And my eyes hurt
From squinting at the newspapers.

We could still make out
A few old trees in the yard.
They take it as it comes.
Separate truths
Do not interest them.

We'll have to run for it, I said,
And had no idea what I meant.
The coming of the inevitable,
What a strange bliss that is,
And I had no idea what she meant.

Late September

The mail truck goes down the coast
Carrying a single letter.
At the end of a long pier
The bored seagull lifts a leg now and then
And forgets to put it down.
There is a menace in the air
Of tragedies in the making.

Last night you thought you heard television
In the house next door.
You were sure it was some new
Horror they were reporting,
So you went out to find out.
Barefoot, wearing just shorts.
It was only the sea sounding weary
After so many lifetimes
Of pretending to be rushing off somewhere
And never getting anywhere.

This morning, it felt like Sunday.
The heavens did their part
By casting no shadow along the boardwalk
Or the row of vacant cottages,
Among them a small church
With a dozen gray tombstones huddled close
As if they, too, had the shivers.

XIV

New Poems

I'm Charles

Swaying handcuffed
On an invisible scaffold,
Hung by the unsayable
Little something
Night and day take turns
Paring down further.
My mind's a ghost house
Open to the starlight.
My back's covered with graffiti
Like an elevated train.
Snowflakes swarm
Around my bare head
Choking with laughter
At my last-minute contortions
To write something on my chest
With my already bitten,
Already bleeding tongue.

Things Need Me

City of poorly loved chairs, bedroom slippers, frying pans,
I'm rushing back to you
Passing every car on the highway,
Searching for you with my bright headlights
Down the dark, empty streets.

O you heartless people who can't wait
To go to the beach tomorrow morning,
What about the black-and-white photo of the grandparents

You are abandoning?
What about the mirrors, the potted plants and the
    coat hangers?

Dead alarm clock, empty birdcage, piano I never play,
I'll be your waiter tonight
Ready to take your order,
And you'll be my distinguished dinner guests,
Each one with a story to tell.

One-Man Circus

Juggler of hats and live hand grenades.
Tumbler, contortionist, impersonator,
Living statue, wire walker, escape artist,
Amateur ventriloquist and mind reader

Doing all that without being detected
While leisurely strolling down the street,
Buying a newspaper on some corner,
Bending down to pat a blind man's dog,

Or sitting across from your wife at dinner,
While she prattles about the weather,
Concentrating instead on a trapeze in your head,
The tigers pacing angrily in their cage.

Lingering Ghosts

Give me a long dark night and no sleep,
And I'll visit every place I have ever lived,
Starting with the house where I was born.
I'll sit in my parents' dimmed bedroom
Straining to hear the tick of their clock.

I'll roam the old neighborhood hunting for friends,
Enter junk-filled backyards where trees
Look like war cripples on crutches,
Stop by a tree stump where Grandma
Made roosters and hens walk around headless.

A black cat will slip out of the shadows
And rub herself against my leg
To let me know she'll be my guide tonight
On this street with its missing buildings,
Missing faces and few lingering ghosts.

Ventriloquist Convention

For those troubled in mind
Afraid to remain alone
With their own thoughts,
Who quiz every sound
The night makes around them,

A discreet tap on the door,
A whispered invitation
To where they have all gathered
In a room down the hall
Ready to entertain you

In a voice of your parents,
The pretty girl you knew once,
One or two dead friends
All pressing close to you
As if wishing to share a secret,

The one with slick black hair
Leaning into your face,
Eyes popping out of his head,
His mouth hanging down
Like a butcher's bloody scale.

The Future

It must have a reason for concealing
Its many surprises from us,
And that reason must have something to do
With either compassion or malice.

I know that most of us fear it,
And that surely is the explanation
We've never been properly introduced,
Though we are neighbors

Who run into each other often
By accident and then stand there
Speechless and embarrassed,
Before pretending to be distracted

By some children walking to school,
A pigeon pecking at a pizza crust
Next to a hearse filled with flowers
Parked in front of a small, gray church.

Softly

Lay the knife and fork by your plate.
Here, where it's always wartime,
It's prudent to break bread unobserved,
Take small sips of wine or beer
Sneaking glances at your companions.

June evening, how your birds worry me.
I can hear them rejoicing in the trees
Oblivious of the troubles that lie ahead.
The fly on the table is more cautious
And so are my bare feet under the table.

Hundreds of bloody flags fleeing at sunset
Across the darkening plains.
Some general leading another army into defeat,
While you pour honey over the walnuts,
And I wait my turn to lick the spoon.

The Starry Sky

Taken as a whole, it's a mystery.
An apparent order concealing a disorder
That would shake us to the core
Were we ever to grasp its senselessness,
Its infinite, raging madness,

Which, for all we know, may be contagious
And explains our terror
At seeing these crowds at the end of day
Convinced a murderer or a lunatic
We'll be hearing about on the late news
Strolls among them now peacefully,

Or so I was telling the old Mrs. Murphy
Who was on her way to church
To pray for the soul of her dead husband,
Who she suspected was in hell
And needed to hear her voice as he burned.

Solitude in Hotels

Where you went to hide from everyone
In a city people visit for other reasons,
In a room with a Don't Disturb sign
Left on the door day and night,
While you sat around in your underwear
Staring at the dead TV screen for hours,

Waiting for after midnight to sneak
Past the desk clerk in the lobby and visit

Some ill-lit dive in the neighborhood
For a beer or two and a bite to eat
Then a walk along dark, deserted streets
In no hurry and no direction in mind,

Slipping back into bed toward daybreak
To lie awake listening to the rain,
While the leaves outside the window
Turn the color of fire, the one you read
Was started by some boy in church
To impress his pale and silent girlfriend.

In the Egyptian Wing of the Museum

Against a coffin thickly ornamented
With paintings representing
The burial rites and duties of the soul
They undid each other's buttons
With all of their fingers on fire.

He, upright like an unicyclist
Going up a pyramid.
She, like a white dove fluttering
In the hands of a magician
Performing at a mortician's convention,

While the dog-headed god
Weighed a dead man's heart
Against a single feather,
And the ibis-headed one
Made ready to record the outcome.

Grandpa's Spells

I hate to hear birds sing
Come spring, the wood turn green
And little flowers sprout
Along the country roads.

Bleak skies, short days,
And long nights please me best.
I like to cloister myself
Watching my thoughts roam

Like a homeless family
Holding on to their children
And their few possessions
Seeking shelter for the night.

And I love most of all knowing
I'm here today, gone tomorrow,
The dark sneaking up on me,
To blow out the match in my hand.

Trouble Coming

One saw signs of it in certain families.
The future was like an unfriendly waiter
Standing ready to take their dinner order
From a menu they could not read.

To look without understanding was their lot
While a salesman in the TV store
Kept changing channels too quickly
For them to retain a single image.

The little flags freshly posted in a cemetery
Said nothing as they hung listlessly
In the early-summer breeze,
Not that anybody particularly noticed.

The sunset over the approaching city
Was like a banquet in a madhouse
The inmates were happily setting on fire
Just as our train ducked into a tunnel.

Nothing Else

Friends of the small hours of the night:
Stub of a pencil, small notebook,
Reading lamp on the table,
Making me welcome in your circle of light.

I care little the house is dark and cold
With you sharing my absorption
In this book in which now and then a sentence
Is worth repeating in a whisper.

Without you, there'd be only my pale face
Reflected in the black windowpane,
And the bare trees and deep snow
Waiting for me out there in the dark.

The Foundlings

Time's hurrying me, putting me to the test
To picture to myself what comes next.
My mind is eager. I no longer plead with it
To keep still so we can get some rest.
We've been this way far too long now.

Like newborn twins, left side by side
On the same church steps by their mother
For some pious early riser to find us,
And either give a shout or take us home,
We'll stay here comforting each other.

Soon now these stone steps will turn pink
And the pigeons and the sparrows
Will fly down to them in search for crumbs
The blind old men who beg here for alms
Let drop as they ate their bread in the dark.

Strange Feast

It makes my heart glad to hear one of these
Chirpy little birds just back from Mexico —
Or wherever it is they spend their winters —
Come and sit in a tree outside my window.

I want to stay in bed all morning
Listening to the returning ones greet the friends
They left behind, since in their rapture
At being together, I find my own joy,

As if a festive table was being set in the garden
By two composed and somber women
Clad in dresses too light for this time of year,
Mindful every glass and fork is in its proper place,

Leaving me uncertain whether to close my eyes,
Or to hurry in shorts over the old snow
And make sure the dishes they've laid out
Are truly there to be savored by one like me.

In a Dark House

One night, as I was dropping off to sleep,
I saw a strip of light under a door
I had never noticed was there before,
And both feared and wanted
To go over and knock on it softly.

In a dark house, where a strip of light
Under a door I didn't know existed
Appeared and disappeared, as if they
Had turned off the light and lay awake
Like me waiting for what comes next.

INDEX OF TITLES AND FIRST LINES